outside
inside

helen ellery

Photography by Jonathan Rose

how to bring the

outside
inside

let your home reflect the seasons

conran
OCTOPUS

First published in 2004 by **Conran Octopus Limited**
a part of Octopus Publishing Group
2–4 Heron Quays, London E14 4JP
www.conran-octopus.co.uk

British Library Cataloguing-in-Publication Data.
A catalogue record for this book is available from the British Library.

ISBN: 1 84091 401 7

Printed in China

PUBLISHING DIRECTOR Lorraine Dickey
ART DIRECTOR Chi Lam
EXECUTIVE EDITOR Zia Mattocks
ART EDITOR Valerie Fong
EDITOR Siobhán O'Connor
PRODUCTION MANAGER Angela Couchman

For my grandma, Muriel Jenkins, where it all started …

contents

introduction

This book is designed to inspire, to allow the reader to imagine a world completely different from the one they inhabit and, furthermore, one that is perfectly achievable. It is as much an interior design book as a manifesto for a way of life. Where minimalism was a suggested antidote to the pressures of modern living by stripping away all the stressful elements of the spaces we live in, my prescription is an altogether more comfortable one, a prescription that is much purer and one which is based on that fundamental emotion that loves the beauty of nature, the outdoors – literally back to our roots.

My childhood was spent in a house with a garden, a garden with flowers, lawns, a vegetable plot, trees that bore fruit, hedges, a greenhouse, a shed, compost, picket fences, scents of seasonal blooms and the joy of seasonal vegetables and fruits. The memory of it has remained with me and formed the kernel of the idea that became both my business, The Plot London, and this book.

OPPOSITE: The season is spring and I have forget-me-nots in my pocket! A trip to the garden yields a voluptuous harvest of inspirations. This tiny bundle of delicate blooms came home with me and gave me many ideas. What will be in your pocket? What is your inspiration? And how will you re-create it?

THIS PAGE: Do not just look at the big picture; notice the little happenings, too. This apple blossom is a tiny little growth, but as important as any observation – and an important design idea for me.

When I came to live in the city, I was committed to a completely different way of life, one where gardens, trees, flowers and the pleasure of work on the land transformed into a small backyard, municipal parks and supermarket produce. I decided to re-create that nostalgic garden environment in my own home using the wonderful elements of the outdoors.

My work and body may be in the city, a fast-moving business environment with traffic and noise, concrete and asphalt, tower blocks, litter, flurry and the scents of the urban culture, but my heart and mind are always yearning for the memory of my country upbringing. As part of my decision to live in the city, I made a conscious effort to create my own country environment, bringing the outside in by using visual references to the outdoors and garden. When I look out of my window, I could be peeking over a trompe-l'oeil hedge blind (shade) instead of on to an apartment block. In the summer this could change to a life-size painting on fabric of glorious lupins in full bloom. My bed throw is reversible; spring and summer fields on one side and autumn and winter on the other.

My window boxes come alive with the seasons: strawberries and sea thrift, snowdrops and bluebells, autumn (fall) grasses, and baby Christmas trees lit up in winter.

My home now reflects the beauty of the ever-changing seasons by utilizing interior design concepts that never fail to inspire, comfort and delight. This plot is my home, and as such it moves through the seasons and all their changes.

the plot

So how does this plot business work? It is a cycle that follows nature's cycle of seasons. The seasons are such a joy, and as inspiring as any work of art or wonderful literary piece. I have come to realize that everything that goes on out there in the great outdoors, in the garden, the allotment and countryside, can be mirrored in the method

This book will be your walk from seed to blossom and back again. And nature will be your inspiration.

of artistic creation used for the great indoors. It is so simple really: getting your hands dirty out there and getting them dirty indoors, too; preparing your ground for the coming seasons – preparing your home for your ideas; planting the seeds – implementing your ideas; cultivating your seeds and propagating your cuttings – moving your ideas on and applying them seasonally. The rest of this book is all about how you take your seeds and cultivate them into a harvest of brilliant and wonderful interior designs.

OPPOSITE: The allotment with its raised beds is a little fruit, vegetable and flower factory of seasonal inspiration. The industry of this place can be paralleled in your home design. The process of growth outside can be reflected within your home.

THIS PAGE: These jolly seed packets decorate my studio wall. Colours, textures, smells, flowers, fruits and vegetables all muddle together. This is truly where it all starts; these are really packets of ideas.

Thompson & Morgan
AUBERGINE
Black Enorma F1 Hybrid
HUGE FRUITS IN ABUNDANCE

Thompson & Morgan
CAULIFLOWER
All the Year Round
BRITAIN'S MOST POPULAR

Thompson & Morgan
NASTURTIUM
Peach Melba

Thompson & Morgan
RUNNER/POLE BEAN
Desiree
STRINGLESS AND WHITE FLOWERS

Mr. Fothergill's
LUPIN
Russell Lupin Mixed

Thomps
TOMA

SWEET PEA
Fragrantissima

Thompson & Morgan
CABBAGE
Golden Acre

SUTTONS
HERB
MINT

PANSY
Winter Flowering Mixed
BEDDING
CHEERFUL MIXTURE

Thompson & Morgan
VIOLA
Bowles Black

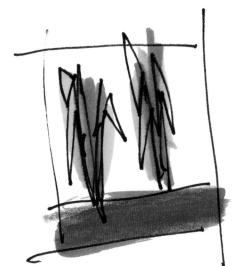

seeds

seed unit of reproduction of a plant capable of developing into another such plant; beginning; offspring.

These tiny, wayward seeds are within you. You are the source of your ideas and inspirations. Whatever you do and whatever you see about you, anywhere and at any time, will form the basis of how you want to create your plot. Trees, flowers and plants through the seasons are literally dressing for the occasion, and how you see them, which ones are your favourites, which

If your home is your plot, your allotment of creativity, then you contain the seeds, the origin of all your inspirations and design ideas.

colours, scents and textures, will give you an idea for your home.

Crucial to keeping your seeds is a little notebook or sketchpad. This is an essential part of your design process because it provides a constant reference of all the goings-on, sightings, thoughts and ideas throughout the year. You will gain great pleasure from jotting notes and sketching on the bus or train, and looking at them when you get home to find out if you have the basis for an idea. Gather cuttings from magazines, articles, photographs and scraps that inspire you. Keep them in a file or folder for your information, as you will need them all in the coming stages of your designs.

This loose scrapbook of ideas and drawings, notes and cuttings will be the foundation for your concept and for your own plot in your own home, so be alert and throw nothing away. There is no need to be precious about how you keep your seeds, no need to be tidy at this stage. Just do not lose it, as it is the very beginning of something marvellous.

These seeds are personal and original. The way that you see, touch and smell is all about you. From this you will design and create something that is completely yours. So take nothing for granted; look up, down and around; keep your senses about you in your search for the seeds of your lovely creations. Remember your notebook, and stuff it with sketches and notes, bits and bobs, messy and rough …

Remain aware of nature as it is to be found in the city, and all the plants, trees and growths will inspire and help you with thoughts and ideas – your seeds. A normal, everyday walk to work, to the corner store or just a simple stroll can yield the most inspiring and exciting observations. You may notice an odd shoot of grass or an unlikely flower growing between the paving stones or creeping out of the rubble on a building site. Even in the most typical and seemingly mundane everyday routines there are always little inspirations and ideas. Pick up your treasures, leaves, weeds and flowers, and press them.

chocolate
pieces

strawberry
milkshake

toffee
melt'n'set

boiling
Jam
(raspberry)

sponge

THIS PAGE: This jumble and clutter of samples and fabrics, workbooks and sketchpads represents the exciting early stage of your design, its beginnings. Make a blooming mess, get stuck in, rummage for inspiring things and start scribbling. You never know when those seeds will germinate and grow.

THIS PAGE: The earth that we see all around us is the fundamental substance for the growth of all your wonderful produce. And here is the empty space ready for the same planning, preparation and toil – anything could happen here.

land

land solid part of the earth's surface, ground; solid expanse of country; landed property.

While you are quietly getting on with gathering your seeds, you are going to need to find somewhere to plant them. Whether you live in the countryside or the city, in a house, apartment or studio, a big space or a tiny space, old or new, this is the place that you want to create and design. Most importantly, however, this is your land, or your plot.

Are you happy with how it functions? Do you use your space efficiently? What material is your home made of? How old is it? Does it have a history? Is the area you live in historically interesting?

Make plans and sketches of your space – your land – as it is. Specify each room's existing function and utility

Identify, understand and research your space. This is your land. This is where you will plant your seeds of inspiration and watch them grow.

positions, plumbing (bathroom and toilet, sinks, taps (faucets) and so on), electrical services (sockets, light fixtures, appliances), heating, fireplaces, wall, ceiling and floor materials, existing furniture ... Simply and clearly look at what you have and how it works. You will make better decisions in the long run if you know where and how you live from the outset.

I have lived in many different types of home, from my childhood in Wales and Bristol to where I live now in London. The apartment that I lived in before I started The Plot was really just a big, empty shell in an old shoe factory in East London. It was my first experience of using space efficiently, but with a concept. I took the time to understand the history of the building and the area. I tried to develop a real feel for the space as it was and how I wanted it to be. The end result was a utilitarian simplicity which was sympathetic both to the area and to the building, but importantly one that was personal and livable, not fashionable or clinical.

When I moved to my current house, I had a different space, of a different age and size, with, above all, a completely new concept and idea of how I wanted to live within that space. I still wanted it to be sympathetic to its history, but at the same time practical and modern. I had my notebook and the seeds of ideas to make a blueprint of how I wanted to live and the land, or space, in which to do it.

The point is, this is your allotment. It is your patch and plot. Mark out your needs and requirements – beds and patches, paths and borders for your creative crops. The design and layout will always be fundamental to your ideas, and anything is possible with good planning and research.

OPPOSITE: A tracing of an old ordnance survey map of my parents' house in the country, laid over a large piece of chequered doll's house flooring paper. The result mixes the idea for my kitchen floor with the plan of the country land.

THIS PAGE: Once you have gathered your thoughts, ideas and seeds, the germination process is quite natural. I get my pens, crayons and equipment out to start germinating. Once you get going it is like starting to write a story – you will find it an exciting journey.

germination

germination process of sprouting or budding; first growth. Once you have collected your seeds and come to understand your land, you can plant out and get germination under way.

The process of germination for your ideas or seeds is the realization that you may be on to something. It is the emergence of a really good thought that has the capacity to go further and grow. The seed from which my business grew, for instance, proved wonderful for me as it had such a lot of possibilities

Germination is the twinkle of an idea, the moment when your seeds begin to sprout from thoughts and inspiration into thoughts and plans.

that I was never stuck for solutions to problems because the original concept, or seed, was so thorough and true.

This is another stage where your notebooks come to the fore. They are the storehouse for your seeds, but they are also the place where those same seeds can make the transition from dormancy to germination. I get ideas in some of the most unlikely of places and at the strangest times. Whenever I do, I usually have my little notebook handy to jot down even the slightest whim or thought. In fact, I had a very important germination moment when I first came up with the idea for The Plot. Originally a concept for an office space, the brief was quite open, and all that was required was a new take on the working environment. I decided to create an environment that was distinctly 'un-officey', a place that people actually wanted to go to work in because it was an encouraging and inspiring environment, but one that also felt different and comfortable. I wanted the outdoors, the garden and the land, to be the concept. I wanted it to be a place in which you would rather be, instead of simply a place in which to work.

The thought of a more nature-orientated space seemed lovely. It made sense – and from that little seed it started to germinate. The seed was a simple little idea. I had been away for the weekend in the country, where I had picked flowers, dug up vegetables, worked in the tool shed and greenhouse, added to the compost, had a few words with a slug or two, sat quietly in the long grass looking out over the horizon of rolling hills, listened to the cuckoo and smelled the grass being cut. It was the thought that I would have to come back to work in the most uninspiring, clinical, soulless environment, with everybody crammed together in little personality-less cubicles, with no attention to needs or happiness, that made me want the outdoors at, on and around my desk. I wanted to bring the outside into my city world.

OPPOSITE: That tiny seed from your tiny packet popped into a little compost in a terracotta pot has sprouted a healthy, sturdy, unique seedling. Its germination has taken place as your idea has sprouted.

cultivation

cultivation preparing and using soil for crops; applying oneself to improving or developing, paying attention to. Cultivation in the garden environment is all about knowing your soil and growing patterns, all about preparation and labour for knowledge. It is about moving things on. You can translate this theory into the practical, useful process that takes your germinated seeds or ideas and elevates them to the next stage.

Cultivation is where you put your ideas down, sketching, measuring and designing. This is where you encourage your ideas to grow.

Now that you are thinking about how to use all your seeds, how to prepare and cultivate your soil, it is time to get out your big sketchpads, to start taking ideas and making them live. This is still a rough playtime, a time for trial and error. A good technique is to use tracing or typo paper to draw over your existing plans and sketches, and just keep experimenting with how you see things in your home, your plot. You are starting to design now, to take the next step.

THIS PAGE: The fleshy spirals of cabbage and lettuce, fresh, spring-green and pert, cultivate an idea for a cushion cover. This sketch in my sketchbook later prompted me to buy a particular cushion.

This book reflects a way of living which I have subconsciously cultivated ever since moving to the city. I missed the simplicity and beauty of nature, its cycles, its seasons, so now I bring the outside inside in any way that I can.

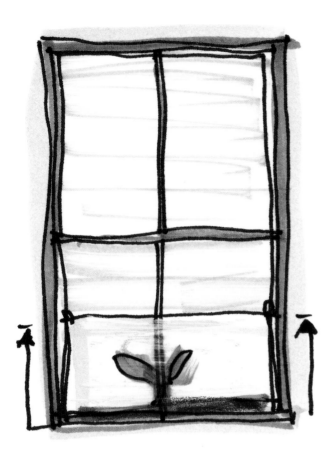

'growing' reverse roman blind

This blind (shade) is a cultivated idea still in sketch stage, but it is a good example of how you can progress any thought or inspiration. The roller blind pulls up and slips over individual hooks, giving the painted illustration of a seedling growing on a sheer organza fabric a feeling of growth. It is a lovely idea and one that I will put into practice one day. You could try other planting ideas – lawn, grass or unfolding fern. The point is to illustrate progress and growth.

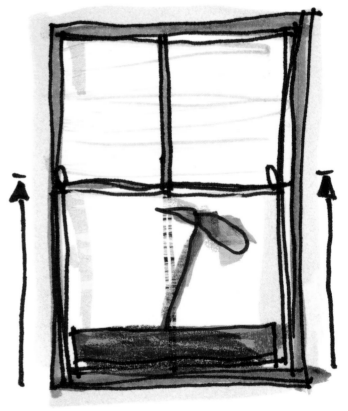

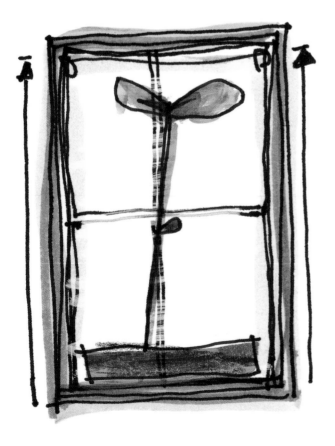

propagation

propagate breeding or reproducing from parent stock. The propagating of your ideas from the seeds and cuttings of your creativity is where you see all your thoughts and inspirations generating more ideas, as one leads to the next. A good method for propagating your ideas is to gather them and concentrate them into visual stories. These are called 'mood boards' and are essential to help you keep track of what it is you

You have germinated your seeds. Now is the time to propagate your ideas and watch them reproduce and proliferate in your living space.

are trying to achieve and remind you of what your concept is. They prevent you from drifting into a world of fluffy thought.

Ideally you will have collated quite a bundle of images and cuttings that have grabbed your attention over your seed-gathering time. The best way to start is to put together your overall concept, your theme or big idea – in this case what your plot is – in a collection of images. You are summing up all that inspires you on just

OPPOSITE: Narcissi's aroma and perkiness combine to make a rare treat. These daffodils have come from my window box. I grew these plants from dry little bulbs, and now they are so successful that they can be divided and planted out again. In much the same way, your ideas will reproduce and multiply.

one board. This is quite tricky, as you will have lots and lots of choice and will have to ruthlessly weed them out.

Buy a selection of foam board from any graphic or art materials store – A1 is a good size to use for the overall plot concept; A2 is better for offshoot boards. You will also need a can of spray-mount, a scalpel and blades (be careful), and a clean, soft cloth. Now you can spray-mount your images onto the board. Set some images in relief with board upon board for impact to create a more interesting effect if you want, rather than using just a single layer of foam board.

Select your essential images and arrange them loosely on the board to give an overall picture. A few simple images are more effective than lots and lots crammed into one area. For me, the plot would be images of soil, lawn, growth (a seedling or bud), a flower and a greenhouse. Remember, the quality of the image and its particular effect on you are the essence. With one look you should see the inspiration for your plot.

Now take cuttings from your concept and produce new shoot ideas (your offshoot boards). You could create mood boards for the seasons and what they mean to you. Make a room-by-room set of boards for mood or for product samples – fabrics, flooring options, wallpapers, paints, and so on. A word of warning: remember to keep your feet planted in some kind of reality. This concept is a subtle and delicate one, so no gimmicks or shortcuts.

OPPOSITE: My trusty old watering can, Billy, has served me well without so much as a squeak or a leak. It is an essential lifesaver for my propagated plants, delivering refreshment to all that need it. The best thing about the propagation process is that it keeps growing and changing, with you and your ideas.

THIS PAGE: Hearty, rich compost will provide all the ingredients for growth and progress; your compost is your memory and creative mulch.

compost

compost mixture of decayed organic matter used as fertilizer; mixture of soil and other ingredients such as peat or moss used for growing seedlings.

The compost is creative mulch, your ideas past and present. It is about recycling ideas and returning them to the soil to enrich future growth. You can never have too much compost.

Recycle every scrap of available material, and value your ideas and memories as if they were gold dust.

Compost is what keeps your ideas and inspiration healthy and alive. It allows them to thrive and be reborn, to be reworked and reused.

Remember, however, to nurture a life-giving, good-quality, healthy compost. Learn to know instinctively what are your good and fruitful ideas. Keep turning over and feeding your ideas, layering them to make the ideal mix to nourish and enhance your plot.

Everything that you are and think of is a unique mixture – your present, your past and your future aspirations. Do not discard the essences as overworked or spent, yet remember to ensure that you are moving and growing, too. Take care to expand your thoughts and look deeper. Think above and below the obvious; look around for change and atmosphere.

Please keep your sketchbooks and notes alive. Continue collecting both your past and your present. Look at what is ahead of you, and remain inspired by the things behind you. Change and progress are all about what you learn from your past and how you put it into your future.

I always get excited at the scents of the seasons. The first narcissi always makes me feel hopeful and optimistic at the coming of spring; the real garden rose, sweet peas and the evocative smell of cut grass at the height of summer; a proper old-fashioned Christmas tree that is the epitome of a nostalgic time; damp leaves and bonfires, carving out pumpkins in the autumn – all are symbols of my past. I can now add big puddles in the road, snow in the local park, piles of leaves on the kerb and weeds poking up through gaps in the pavement to these, and there will be more to come. I add to my compost daily and will keep changing my plot because of it.

My lawn carpet is about to be changed to a dandelion meadow or even a peony bed – brilliant yellow or shocking pink sweeping through the hall will soon replace the grass – it was time for a change, and I had the inspiration long ago. This may seem a bit of a tiny compost connection, but it is all part of the same theory: keep your ideas alive and changing. In fact, I might not even have carpet at all. I will just have to wait to see what there is to get me going …

THIS PAGE: I like to pin up the fabric samples that I have gathered for each season. In this way I can gain an overall picture of the season in just one look – a mass of texture and colour. Pictured here is the winter-berry red theme.

pests

pest troublesome or annoying person or thing; insect or animal that is destructive to plants.

There are many problems or pests that can trip you up, many slugs in your lettuces and greenfly all over your sweet peas, but with patience and the best possible understanding of your problems the drama may be short-lived. Minimize errors as much as you can by planning and preparing, trying out ideas on a small scale first. Research as much as possible before you commit.

Pests are the inevitable problems that occur on your creative path. Just try to keep them under control, and learn from the experience.

You are bound to make mistakes and get it wrong, but it is really OK. You are exploring and hopefully having fun! Just as your sketchbook will be full of terrible sketches and silly ideas which you nevertheless keep as reference and learn from, so, too, your paint colours and ideas may not be all that you had in mind. Nothing is set in stone – except the kitchen sink and fixtures, which will be costly errors and so require real thought. Everything else is your palette and can be redone. Be brave, think the best and learn from mistakes.

OPPOSITE: I have only a very small area to grow anything in my tiny London plot – window boxes, yard and terrace – but the devastation that certain pests can wreak is quite phenomenal. Keep a weather eye out, both outside and inside.

While you are on your creative adventure, you are bound to meet your share of slugs and snails. Do not become despondent – stick to your path!

peeking-over-the-hedge blind This blind (shade) was one of my first ideas. It is meant to be an intricate, delicate layer of embroidered hedge on a fabric panel. I have made several attempts, but I really need a professional embroiderer or a few years' experience to succeed with it – an endearing pest.

THIS PAGE: My 'greenhouse' is the messiest room in the house. It is a riot of colour and texture, with a jumble of things on the go – a place of continual planting, cultivation, propagation and production, always blossoming with ideas. It is a happy place and the heart of my plot.

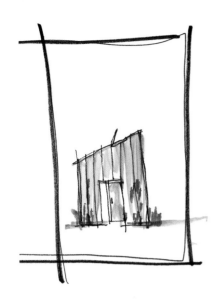

the greenhouse

greenhouse a light structure, with sides and roof made mainly of glass, used for rearing plants.

The greenhouse is where you can exercise your creativity and develop and grow your seedlings of ideas. Personalize your space. Surround yourself with favourite things which you have gathered over the years and which have special meaning and special power to spark your inventive genius.

Get organized: use files or portfolios for your drawings; allocate a shelf, drawer or storage box for keeping samples of paint and fabrics; and file all your paperwork, quotes and costings. Most of all, make sure that you have plenty of space to lay out your work and turn your ideas into reality. This is your work room: pin up your ideas on the walls so that you can monitor your progress and keep experimenting; assemble swatch boards with your sketches and drawings alongside samples of fabrics and paints, floor coverings and treatments

The greenhouse is the heart of your plot. It is the place to propagate seedlings and cuttings, a place for growing your ideas and plans.

that have caught your eye. Make the room alive with thoughts and ideas. Being surrounded by inspirations will help to keep those very ideas fresh and growing.

You will need as much natural light as possible; some kind of task lighting for close work is also vital, as well as a sturdy desk or table as big as you can get. A comfortable chair is a necessity, as is a lot of storage and shelving.

While this room is very much a functioning work area, it should also still be a part of your concept for your home. Do not neglect this space; it, too, can be in tune with the seasons, so if you have curtains, cushions, chairs, and space for blooms and plants, then change them with the seasons as you will do in the rest of your living environment. Bunting works well – it softens the edge of a practical space and makes it more inviting. Keep changing it, of course, perhaps with fresh flowers that will keep the air sweet and the atmosphere welcoming.

My greenhouse is on the ground floor of my house; it is light and cluttered, but has lots of space. It is where I go to work and put pen and crayon to paper; I make things there, call suppliers and read reference material. It is not the shed where I retreat for those special just-cannot-think moments; it is the creative part of my plot. I did, however, deliberately build a separate entrance to this studio on the ground and basement floors, so that the two spaces, living and work, would be clearly divided.

OPPOSITE: This greenhouse has served my family with various fruits and vegetables for years. It is both a powerhouse of produce and a haven. Grapes hang from the windowpanes, and a musky, earthy smell lingers on your clothing well after you have left. It is a very happy, warm and productive place.

the shed

shed a one-storey structure utilized for storage or shelter, or as a workshop, and so on.

The shed can mean and therefore consequently be different things to different people. It can be the place to store your tools and equipment, or a place to go to when you think that you are all out of ideas or inspiration – the real shed or the fantasy shed. If it is a practical place, then make it work: hang your tools, store your fabrics, books and magazines with care. If you are off to the fantasy shed, try a place that inspires and yet calms you, one where you can forget your worries and breathe again.

Whatever you choose to make your shed mean to you, and wherever you choose to site it, make sure that it meets all of your needs.

I have a lot of 'sheds'. One is in the basement of the house, where I store all my working materials, books, paints and tools – there is a warm, secluded feel to the room and yet it still meets all my practical needs.

OPPOSITE: This rather special shed contains a multitude of tools and wonderful garden equipment. A very magical place and a very hard-working one, it is imbued with the smells of cut grass, oil, creosote and wood.

When I am in Cornwall, I hear the seagulls, eat pasties, walk on the cliffs and climb over boulders of granite, walk Bert and Mabel on the stretches of white sand, and feel the salty air beat on my face. Suddenly I am excited and rejuvenated again.

THIS PAGE: For me, Cornwall is my fantasy shed, a big, lovely, reclusive place and one that never fails to take me away from the clutter of the city and its draining sapping of thought. Pictured here is the walk along the coast to Zennor, near Porthmeor. It is where I gather my thoughts and gather inspiration. It is pure air and freedom, and a very special place indeed.

production

production total yield; things produced.

Harvest Festival and Christmas are particular times that mean all those thoughts and ideas, experiments and efforts are now going to bear fruit. You are going enjoy your own designs; you have the season in your home now ... the window boxes are festive with mini fir trees, or you are gazing at your holly bush blind, maybe sitting in the evergreen chair with a cosy snowdrift throw

Production is the harvest of your ideas, the things you have made, the fruits and blossoms of your ideas and inspirations.

over you, or snuggling up at night with the two-season eider-down in its winter combination and gazing at your snowfall fairy lights. It is yours and all your own interpretation. Revel in the fruits of your labour ... But what next?

It took me a year to make my plot, from the first seed of an idea to actually sitting down on my comfortable tweedy sofa and sipping a restorative cup of tea, then a small sherry! I had completely converted the empty,

OPPOSITE: Bountiful Christmas marks both the end of the year and a celebration of your creativity. This season is production heaven: throws, window treatments, chair covers, cushions and bunting are all an indulgence of the wintertime.

derelict shell into a live/work space. It was my living space, my workplace and above all my home. It felt like a haven or sanctuary. It was everything of which I had dreamed.

But the best was still to come, as, season by season, I would be able to change my interior to match the flow of nature outside. My window boxes would take me from snowdrop to pumpkin; my chair cover would be lupin pink or evergreen; the seats in the studio would look like giant soft felt terracotta pots; the lawn would always be green and never need mowing.

I am at home in my own little allotment of creativity and far from the harshness of the city in ambience, if not in actual distance. I have been through the processes of planting, growing and harvesting. My home is my plot, and like nature it is continually growing and changing.

Now that you have all your produce, remember that it is just one season – there will be many more to come. I keep the produce fresh and pack it carefully when I put it away for a season change, as it may be coming back out again the next year. But I also have annuals that are simply thrown away at the end of the season. Bunting and blooms or certain plants are simply replaced the next time they are needed. Having finished a whole year of produce, try not to give up, thinking that it is all done. Start again; think of new ways to bring the seasons in. Change the theme of your blinds; replace that evergreen chair cover. Keep your production line going!

OPPOSITE: Pinks are simple, rather old-fashioned, traditional flowers which give out a heavy, thick scent that lingers in the air. Their flesh-like hue makes a lovely wall colour, and the frill of the petals provides a fabric inspiration.

the groundwork

The groundwork is the underlying basis or preparatory work. It is the formative stage on which plans and options are based. This is the most important part of the outside-inside process, as it sets the nature palette from which your creations grow. You must get your basics right. To make your plot a truly genuine and original interior, the crucial groundwork must be laid; walls, ceilings, floors, fixtures and fittings, and details – all these have to be considered. When you

Deciding on the look and feel of the permanent features of your house sets the scene for all your ideas.

have prepared your plot to your satisfaction, your designs can grow from it and blossom. An amalgamation of cultivation, propagation and all the preparation that has gone into your designs, this should not be some dreadful, grim process of strict rules. But it is about all the big, basic stuff: this is the time to get down to the nitty-gritty of it all – the practicalities.

OPPOSITE: Spring planting in the family garden with Bert. He likes to be involved in everything I do, but especially things that involve digging and mud. He is quite accomplished at carving deep holes in the earth.

walls

Once you are confident that the rooms you have are right for your needs, that you have a good connection between the rooms you use most and have all the space and light that you want, look at the walls as special and beautiful in their own right. Are they made of brick, stone, plaster or perhaps wood? What is your concept overall? What colours, themes and textures are you considering?

I have always used a core colour palette consisting of white, off-white, stone, black and pale natural shades such as green and blue. Using these colours for my walls provides a good, solid background for the seasonal changes that I create with the furnishings and details. In particular, limestone and black are very effective. Vibrant colours such as pumpkin orange, lupin pink, holly-berry red and delphinium blue are all offset brilliantly by these two colours. I will definitely be using more

Generally walls provide the perfect backdrop for your ideas. Develop fresh, exciting ways to make them look great without overpowering.

black in the future – it's dramatic, honest and glamorous. Doors, skirtingboards (baseboards) and ceilings all could do with a splash of black. Glossy and glistening, or matt and chalky are both really exciting and make other colours resonate.

Throughout most of my living space I have used medium to narrow tongue-and-groove with a 'V' groove, which has generated a seaside cottage feel. I initially got the idea to tongue-and-groove after a bit of research; it seemed that the street had a history of tongue-and-groove, and I was compelled to sympathize. It worked well, and painting it has made it seem as if it has always been there, which is just what I wanted in trying to eliminate the dead, developed look that seems so rife in much of today's building work. Often, not an ounce of consideration is given to the history or preservation of good craftsmanship and taste. People are too quick to rip out, gut and destroy, and remove any trace of the past in the pursuit of a quick buck from those who neither know nor care about any other way. But maybe they would, given the choice, avoiding the plastering, PVC windows, laminated floors and kitchen doors that makes one space the same as any other.

In my basement and ground-floor hallway I have bare brick walls, which I rubbed down myself. They are good and real, and alive with texture and warmth. Think before you plaster. But if you do not have an option, look at textured wallpapers or consider good-quality gloss or matt paint. Maybe you could use a map of your favourite area, pasted and varnished for an aged effect. The long stretch of a corridor or hallway can be a great place to try this. So, there is much more to walls than meets the eye. Be original and push the boundaries.

THIS PAGE: This sunny, thoroughly vibrant yellow painted on a top-floor bedroom wall reflects the sun and keeps the room light. OPPOSITE: Painted brick, in your choice of colour, looks effective and clean.

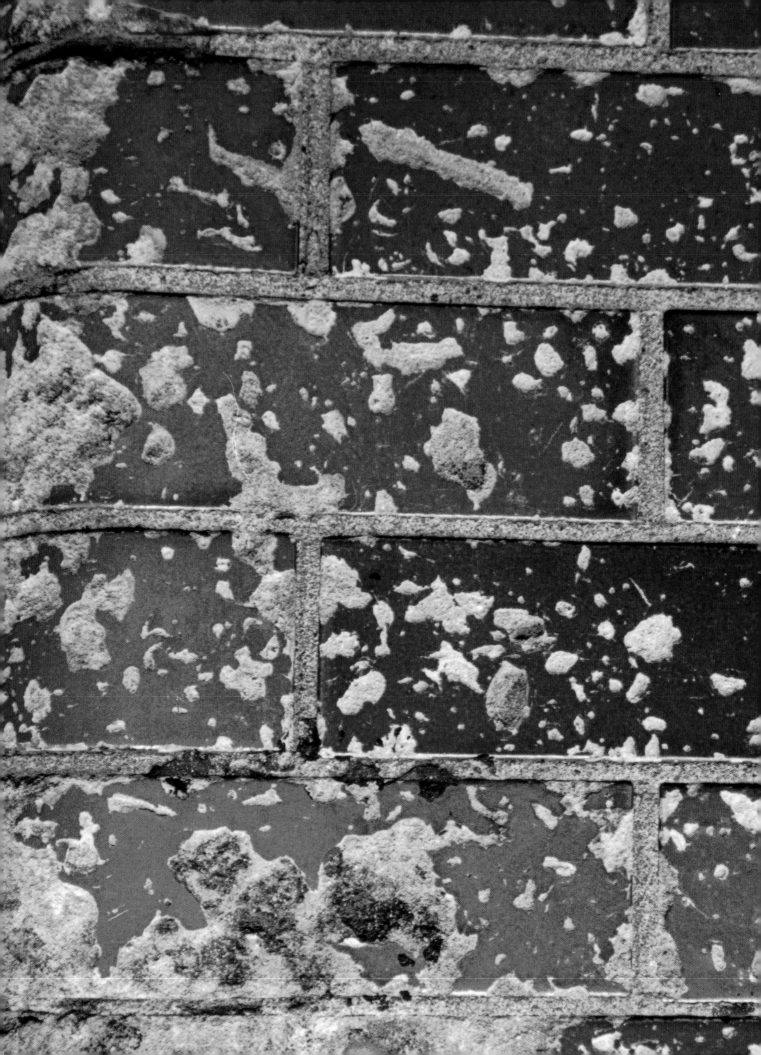

wall influences

BRICK Brick adds tremendous warmth and character to a space. A single wall or two creates a good effect, or you can expose the whole room; however, an all-brick room can be overbearing, dusty and cold if in an older property. Many brick walls outdoors benefit from tree or plant growth. As wonderful as it would be in the interior, this is unlikely. Do not start painting murals or friezes on your brick. It will not look as good as you want, and will grind you down daily with a 'why did I do that?' feeling. And never buy brick wallpaper.

STONE Cornwall has some of the most staggeringly beautiful stone walls, which fit together like jigsaw puzzles and always mesmerize me. Lichens and mosses creep in and out of the gaps, making the wall a work of art. Older properties can offer stone walls, but any kind of replica gives a very unsavoury result. I would prefer to try to simulate the beautiful colours of the stone and/or the texture of the lichens, mosses and so on with paint or rubbed wallpaper, and old plaster left untouched but waxed to a delicate varying sheen.

FENCING Wooden gates, fences and doors are great wall influences. Whether painted or natural, new or old, bashed and battered, wood is a homely, insulating material. Tongue-and-groove wooden walls are a great wall treatment and create a reassuring atmosphere. You can use different widths, thick or thin,

THIS PAGE: Simple painted walls – no fuss and no palaver; just a lovely clean, neutral white space, filled with light and air. **OPPOSITE:** This caramel glazed brick is beautiful and quite commonplace in the part of London where I live.

with a bead or a 'V' groove, either on one wall for an effect or maybe go the whole hog and clad the walls and ceiling for a wonderful lived-in feeling. Paint the wood, or wax or varnish. I prefer a lick of paint, but the wood stretches and shrinks, so be prepared for cracks and splits – nothing to worry about.

HEDGE Box, holly, beech, blackthorn, laurel, yew, hawthorn and privet, topiary … I have a bit of a thing for hedges and use their influence in lots of ways, but for walls I keep their effect to textured wallpaper, an Anaglypta or textured pattern, or even a rough paint wash and wax.

LICHEN AND MOSS Natural flocking, a patchwork of grey, brown, white, green and yellow that cover tree trunks in unpolluted areas, can be compared to old plaster walls, maybe washed with a colour and waxed or matt varnished.

PLANTS AND TREES Think of climbing plants such as ivy, wisteria, clematis, roses, sweet pea, camellia and honeysuckle; and trees and plants such as red-hot poker, thistle, bay and lilac. Their textures and colours yield a stunning overall wall effect. Elegant patterned wallpapers, embossed wallpapers – especially lovely big thick Anaglyptas – are quite magnificent and can re-create the effect of the real thing very well. Stamping is cheap and very easy, and temporary if you use a light water-based paint. You can make a stamp of anything, and to any size, but don't get too literal – make it witty and understated. Less is more in the world of stamping.

THIS PAGE: Wood is as natural and everyday as you can get, but never dull or boring. Warm and cosy, it has timeless charm. **OPPOSITE:** This gorgeous purple was an exact match to a flower that grew in rampant abundance in the garden outside.

wall materials

PAINT There are endless possibilities here: bold, strong colours that bring character and opinion to a room, or neutral, muted shades that stand back and let your belongings take the stage. Colour is a good thing, but bear in mind the whole concept and avoid leaping between very strong colours from one room to the next; the rooms should flow elegantly and never jar.

BARE PLASTER Naked walls can look good in more urban/industrial environments, places where the unfinished look can be at its most effective. Polished or waxed, bare plaster makes for a very unusual and lovely effect.

WOOD Tongue-and-groove, thick or thin, 'V' groove or beaded – the choice seems infinite. Not only can wood be used to hide a multitude of wall messes, including incurable damp spots, but it gives warmth and an insulated feel to your space.

PANELLING If you are fortunate enough to have some history to your home and have wall panelling, do please look after it as it is gorgeous. Natural or painted, a nice bit of panelling gives a room no end of character.

WALLPAPER Wallpaper selection is extensive and fabulous these days, from intriguing textures to colours unimaginable a few years ago. Consider anything that sets your imagination aflutter – from big floral prints to pale stripes or polka dots.

BRICK A simple brick wall or walls is as basic as you can get. It may need to be sealed with some type of sealant if left bare; otherwise, painted brick looks equally appealing.

floors

One of the most fundamental components of the home, flooring brings the space together. I like to connect halls, stairs and landings with one type of flooring. Floors that flow from area to area give a feeling of space and confidence. Coloured or textured flooring can be lovely,

Your flooring should have a subtle background beauty that feels and looks right, integral to the house.

especially when leading off from a rough wooden, slate or tile corridor. Be brave here: steer clear of beige and neutrals.

Wood, rubber, fitted carpet or area rugs, matting, leather, linoleum, stone, granite, brick, terracotta, tile: when it comes to flooring, the choice for function and aesthetic quality is bewildering. Consider how each material looks and makes you feel, and how it would suit the function of each room and the way you live or work within it. Think quality above anything else, and get it fitted by a specialist. Areas of concern in terms of wear and tear are hallways, corridors, stairs and task areas such as the kitchen, bathrooms, and those high-traffic spots near desks, sofas and doors. Living rooms and dining rooms suffer food and drink mishaps. If you have children or pets, consider their potential for mischief, too.

THIS PAGE: Hard-wearing and in unlimited colours, rubber flooring is practical and contemporary.
OPPOSITE: Traditional wooden floorboards are always warm underfoot and immensely practical – and they age beautifully.

flooring influences and materials

BRICK, TILE, TERRACOTTA AND STONE Think of paths and terraces laid in patterns, with weeds and mosses growing in between the stones. Tiles are smoother and more sophisticated than brick; both come in various shapes, sizes and thicknesses and are slippery when wet. Terracotta can come over a bit Mediterranean, so watch it! Big slabs of stone are hard-wearing and easy to maintain as well as beautiful. Granite and slate are particularly striking, but can be cold and hard on your feet.

GRASS AND EARTH The land is a rich source of colours and textures: emerald, lime, moss and yellow greens; rough, lush and mixed grasses; the red oxide, burnt sienna, ochre, grey and brown of soil. Carpet can be dyed whatever colour you like. Also worth considering is poured resin, which is ideal for large working areas, but needs to be applied to a solid concrete base. Natural-fibre flooring can create a sandy loam soil effect.

SNOW AND FROST The best way to reproduce a wintry setting is with painted floorboards – a blue-grey undercoat with a brilliant white topcoat and a rubdown with soft sandpaper. White increases the sense of space, but can be high maintenance.

FLOWERS AND PLANTS Take inspiration from lavender, ferns, gorse and heather – colours that make you feel as if you are walking among heavenly fragrant leaves or your favourite flowers. Richly coloured carpet, rubber or a dense beeswax-fed leather will do the job.

OPPOSITE: Good-quality carpet can be a comfort and reassurance beneath your feet. Choose brave, bold colours and different textures. Avoid the beige safety option; use your imagination and think of nature's colours – lupin pink, grass green, delphinium blue, dandelion yellow or marigold orange.

ceilings

Ceilings, ceilings, ceilings – well, what can you say? Ceilings are the things that you look up at when you cannot sleep, that pancakes get stuck to, that leak and are banged on if whatever is going on upstairs is too loud. Ceilings are dull but necessary and should therefore be accepted for what they are. That does not mean giving up. It is possible to make the ceiling a touch more tasty than normal with a little thought.

What worries me most here, given the concept of this book, is the obvious: that is, ceiling equals sky. Well, it does, and that is nice, but please do not start painting all the ceilings a sky-blue with lovely fluffy white clouds. This is fairy-tale stuff and, although we are being light-hearted, our aim is not the ridiculous. So wait and be smart. When it came to my home, I painted the ceilings the same colour as

With a little effort and care on your part, you can transform the most utilitarian ceiling into a stunning lid.

the walls, which suited. There is never a need, in my opinion, to emphasize ceilings with paint techniques. It looks awful and contrived, so keep it simple, and let light and shade do it naturally. This is important: no gimmicks here, please. Choose neutral colours to match the walls, or strong, individual ones. Think textures – wooden, papered, painted, varnished …

THIS PAGE: If painting the ceiling, I really do prefer to use the same colour as the walls. It looks smart and confident. and keeps warmth in the room. OPPOSITE: Wooden ceilings, natural or painted, are rather lovely. If painted, a matt or gloss finish are both easeful. It helps with sound insulation and makes a room feel as if it has a cosy lid.

ceiling influences and materials

PAINT Different 'feels' to a room can be achieved with the use of different colours, with especially dramatic results on ceilings. A ceiling will seem lower if you use a darker paint colour; conversely, the impression of height is achieved by using a lighter colour. Painting your ceiling white is one of those things you are 'supposed' to do, but it is rather dated (unless you are using very dark colours on the walls, of course). I prefer to make the ceiling colour the same as the walls.

PLASTER AND CORNICING Decorative ceilings are lovely and you are lucky if you have them, but avoid making any more of them than their already wonderful detail. Paint the ceiling one colour, and let natural light play with the shadows.

WOOD I particularly like wooden ceilings. Tongue-and-groove planks painted with a high-gloss finish bestow a really warm, effective atmosphere. Wood has an insulating effect and makes any room feel cosy, in a rather traditional way. Exposed timber ceilings are also gorgeous, whether natural wooden or painted beams. Care should be taken as to where the wooden ceiling is situated as there is a fire-safety issue to be considered.

WALLPAPER If you have a low ceiling already and have wallpapered your walls, wallpaper your ceiling, too – it makes a delightful snug room. High ceilings do not lend themselves as well to wallpaper, so in this situation leave the ceiling painted.

THIS PAGE: A straightforward, simple, painted concrete ceiling. The natural light in the room emphasizes the structural shapes.
OPPOSITE: This beautiful ceiling is a hexagonal plaster moulding and gives a gentle and elegant look. Painting it a chalky white keeps the simplicity, while subtly highlighting the shapes.

fixtures & fittings

THIS PAGE: A high-level cistern is an effective space-saving solution. If your room is small, attention is drawn to the fixtures; make them beautiful and attend to detail. Even a toilet cistern should look good.

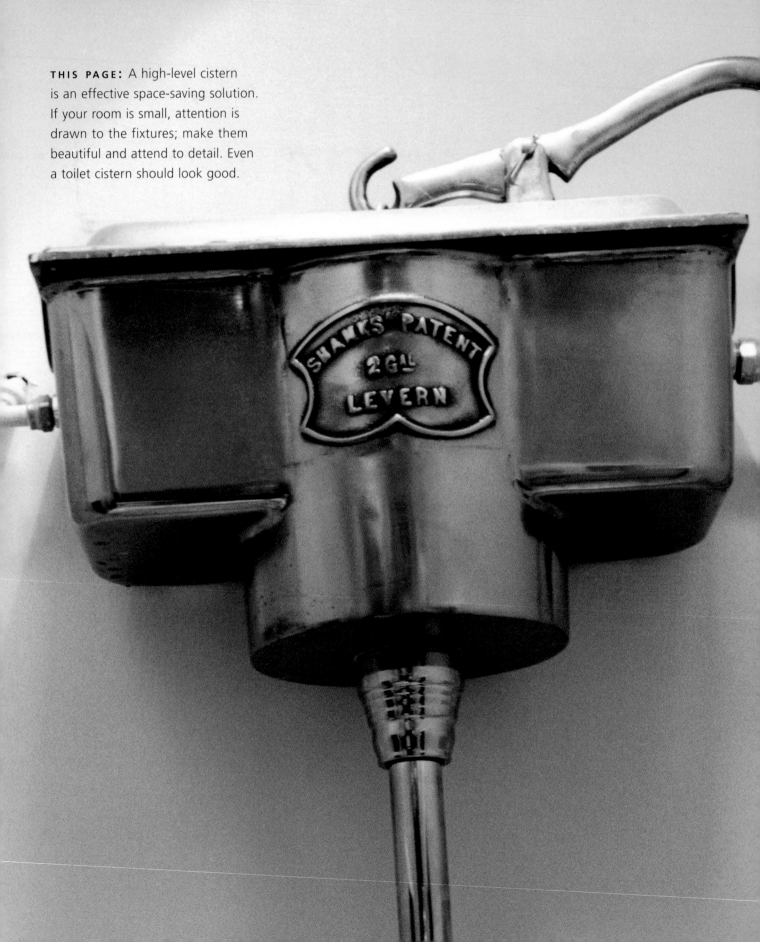

SHANKS PATENT 2GAL LEVERN

bathroom This may be the incorrect term for me, as mine is really more of a shower room. I decided a second bedroom should take preference over a bathroom; I sometimes think that this may not have been a good idea, but rather a 'pest', as I have sorely missed a bath. Still, my shower is a grand affair, a wonderful reclaimed French antique that packs out a mighty flow and looks elegant and in keeping with the house.

Bathrooms are hard-working rooms: they exist to serve a purpose and need to be well thought out. They can still be beautiful at the same time. Planning is crucial. Write down how you use this room. Do you like a shower or bath, or both? How many people will use it? How do you want to heat it? Is it a special room for you to withdraw to or a functional family place that needs to be efficient? Whatever your needs, try to select quality fixtures. I feel an outside-inside bathroom is one that is more sympathetic to a traditional reclaimed style, where the fixtures are a bit beaten up or have a sense of history

The choice of bathroom fixtures is vast – traditional or contemporary, new or reclaimed. Take time when choosing, and think long term.

and originality to them. I like the room to feel like a lost room rediscovered or an outhouse that was long neglected. I also like to hunt for old French bathtubs or sinks, rummage for unusual taps (faucets) and make investigations into weird and wonderful toilets. Try as always to be sympathetic to your home and its era. Keep it simple again, and emphasize detail.

kitchen Whether you love to cook or not, the kitchen is very much the heart of any home. If you have anywhere near a half-decent area, people are always drawn to this natural hub of a house. And so it should be. The kitchen is a place in which to cook, eat, clean and carry out all manner of tasks and chores, and as with the bathroom it should be planned thoughtfully. It needs to supply all the requisite services – food preparation and cooking, perhaps your laundry facilities, storage for your utensils and equipment, maybe a place for eating – but also you want it to be personalized and to reflect your concept.

Do your homework and seek out a particular look. Think about the materials that would suit your kitchen – steel, stone, wood or tile, or a mixture. For me the solution is a traditional feel, with black as a rather unusual paint finish. A good colour combination for kitchen units is a warm sage green or chalky white, black (matt or gloss) and a putty stone colour. Colours that come

In my kitchen old influences have been mixed with modern to impart a feeling of practical nostalgia in a neutral and natural colour scheme.

into the space in products and goods, or personal effects, seem to look better for this neutral background. Steel worktops are wonderful, as are wooden tops. Taps (faucets) and fixtures can be sourced from reclamation yards, and a hard-working oven is at the heart of it all. Store tools on the walls; keep shelving light and open. This room should be relaxed and happy, a place for socializing and creating, so keep it friendly and not clinical.

BREAD

THIS PAGE: A labour of love. I stripped back these wooden stairs, removing countless layers of paint. I wanted to reveal the original pine wood beneath. I think the result is so lovely – soft and natural, warm and comforting. Waxing the finished surface gives it a rich finish, keeping the beauty of the old wood alive.

stairs, windows and doors Umpteen different types and styles of stairs, windows and doors are available, but my choice will always be sympathetic to the house or apartment, its age and its style. This is the framework of your home, and it is better kept as simple and natural as possible. Dabbling in odd styles can make for a very peculiar effect.

My stairs and staircase were in a lovely state of semi-undress when I first saw them, with years of layers of paint of various colours, blues and greens mainly, and the original pine wood peeking through. I decided to strip back all the painted areas, stairs and window frames, then waxed the wood to soften and mellow the tone; it now appears as old and battered as it ever did, but with added warmth. You may want to paint your main areas. If you do, keep colours neutral. That's not to say

These functional parts of the home can be and sometimes are more than plain old function, if just a little thought is implemented first.

that it cannot be bold; just try not to make features out of the fundamentals. They should blend with your home and allow the things that you bring into your home to sing. Think black, white, stone, green and grey – all natural outdoor colours that will look stunning on your doors, stairs or frameworks.

Think about the details as well: what door handles will you use, do you need hooks for hanging clothes, will you have carpet or keep a wooden floor on the stairs? Keep thinking to bring all your fixtures together with your fundamentals.

details

furniture Your living tools, all the things that you sit, eat, work, relax on and fall asleep in, big and little things, useful and just good-looking things ... your furniture will, of course, be existing and hard to part with, but this book will help you adapt and change if you want to. If possible, strip back to the basics and see each item that you possess as a piece that functions and also gives you pleasure. See each item as standing on its own. Let your furniture breathe and have a place.

Clutter is the mass of indecision that says, 'Uuuum?' You actually need very little to give a lot away. All that is yours does not need to be out there shouting about you and your life. You want a part but not the whole of your life laid out for all to see – thoughtful and precious, but selective.

And think about scale. Allegedly, the smaller the space, the smaller the furniture. Well, I think that big stuff in small spaces is better. I have a big clock, a big fridge, a big bookcase, a big sofa and a big old chair, but they fit and do not look cramped. Sometimes the bigger the furniture, the bigger the room feels. That's not to say that you are a giant and need big everything – just the essentials and the effect is fine.

Commit to the things that stand out for you and represent who you are. Be unpretentious in your choices.

THIS PAGE: This smashing old chair has been through the wars, to say the least (I would not rely on it for sitting, but it is fine for books and magazines). I would never think of throwing it out, though. It has the most delightful spearmint paint colour, which has chipped over the years and now looks rather battered, but that is its charm.

THIS PAGE: The platform bed, the greatest storage solution ever. This one is to be found in my spare room. It keeps the room a bedroom, with space to sleep and store in a very small area, providing two functions within one area. It looks great, too, and reminds me of a treehouse.

storage Like most people, I have a lot of 'stuff' – books, linens and personal belongings that can fill rooms, let alone shelves. Much as I try, and I do try, it is hard to dispose of your past and make decisions over what is to go and what is to stay. But it is worth doing. Being more selective about your possessions gives a feeling of clearness and enhances rather than detracts from the things you want to show and enjoy.

There are two types of storage that I have used: built-in and not built-in – rocket science! Basic shelves painted the same colour as the walls is a good solution for books, and books around you is a great feeling, as are the little things. I have postcards, a

In spaces without space, so to speak, storage is very important. Always give it proper consideration and never take shortcuts.

dog and a kennel in tin given to me by a friend, lead farm and country figures, and a collection of green and orange Penguin Classics, among others, and the shelves, which are nice and chunky, are full without looking cluttered. I have a vast old school cupboard, half wood and half glass-door storage. It is a lovely piece and has made the living area complete, as well as being a way of storing and displaying books and bits and bobs.

Other storage in the house is shelved, but the underbed storage is a great success. I have a bed and deep cupboards for linen and clothing in one big structure, and would make this choice again. Where a natural and garden/outdoor-influenced concept can be used, then it is just that – natural.

lighting Bright and unnecessary light makes everything stark and clinical. I prefer light for specific needs or jobs, and shy away from the general blanket-of-light approach. Rooms that require a good light level are those that are used for tasks, such as bathing or cooking, or operating a rotating blade of some sort. All other tasks can be spotted for themselves.

Lighting for living and relaxing should certainly be low-level or warm and understated, not operating-room bright. In the study, keep the light really low-level and spot the study area with a task spotlamp. Think about the requirement for each room, think about dimmers and control, and try to create pockets of light instead of blankets.

One of the greatest things to have happened to my home is the fairy light. I must have at least 30 different sets of fairy lights – large, small, berry red, white, multicoloured, outdoors and indoors. At Christmas and spring I dot little bundles of bulb lights

Lighting is a vital component of a space; it creates mood and a feeling of 'home'. Keep the wattage low and appropriate to the room.

of appropriate colours about the house. The small bedroom glows a welcome when lit with just a fairy-light bundle – although not great for reading in bed, there are bed spotlights over the bedhead to accommodate this.

All in all I have lots of lamps and lots of little light projects, rather than a big single switch. For me it really is the most flexible and delightful way of suiting my needs and fancies.

THIS PAGE: I cannot get enough of fairy lights; they are so versatile. Such wonderful bundles of light, they always create an atmosphere, whatever the season or celebration. I use these red berry lights at Christmas, draped over the studio wall clock. When the main lights are switched off at the end of the day, the room is aglow with holly-berry red light – utterly Christmassy.

the seasons

Each season of the year provides a chance to change and move on to a new situation. Personally, I would not choose to live in a country that was continuously hot – or one that was continuously cold, for that matter – or even one that had just the two choices, hot or cold. I like the subtle differences of the seasons: lively, unpredictable spring; warm and often downright hot and balmy summer; brilliant vibrant autumn (fall); and crisp, chilly, drizzly, gloomy winter. They are all a delight to me, and I anticipate them eagerly.

It is because of our wonderful seasons that we are able to appreciate so much in our outdoor world, in our gardens, backyards, allotments and countryside. Each new season has so much to give to us in terms of inspiration. The older I become, the more I am aware of these seasonal details; more and

We are lucky to have the seasons and their different fashions and ways. Each change over the year keeps us renewed and inspired.

more I seem to appreciate the littlest things. The intricacy of catkins, the tiny sprigs of green popping up in the ground and between paving stones, crocuses in the park, the dazzling colours of autumn leaves, the smell of bonfires, muddy walks in winter – all are so distinctive and very exciting to me.

two-season reversible eiderdown

This eiderdown idea is a good seasonal staple, inspired purely by the simplicity of the earth. One eiderdown is made of a chunky earth-brown jumbo cord representing autumn (fall) and flips over to luxurious thick, soft, white velvet for winter; the second eiderdown shows spring as a simple brown felt with green-tweed striped sprouting within the ridges, while its reverse represents summer in a tactile thick linen in a true grass green. These pieces are basic duvet (continental-quilt) covers really, machine-stitched on to the inserted eiderdown and sealed for ever. Simple but gorgeous, they say a lot about the seasons without trying too hard.

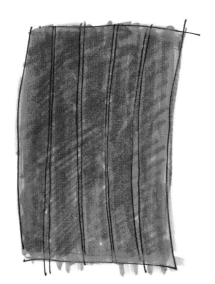

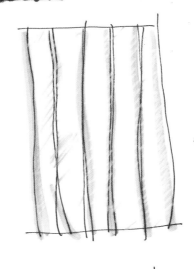

autumn / winter

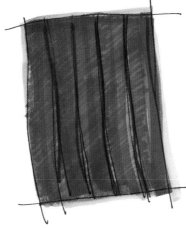

spring / summer

spring

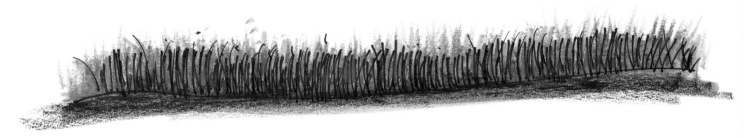

With every season, scent is a big factor in identifying the change from one to the other, but I think spring is probably the most fragrant of all. I can tell immediately the day that spring has arrived. It is difficult to put into words, but it somehow feels as if a big lid has been lifted off the day and there is a lightness and freshness that was not there yesterday, a feeling of optimism and happiness. Everything starts to warm up as the earth begins to defrost from the bleakness of the winter. Certainly, winter does tend to drag on a bit, and at times I would rather spring came a little earlier, say, the beginning of January, so that I could open up the window, take a deep breath and there it is, spring, all big and sexy, fragrant and cheeky. The best thing to do if you are able is to get out into the countryside and look for

spring colours white ✳ various yellows ✳ pale and hot pink ✳ spring greens and limes ✳ lilacs ✳ blues

inspirations further afield. Explore the outdoor world and let spring gently creep up on you – the indescribable green in the trees budding everywhere with innocence and youth, the fruitful and delightful fleeting blossoms, the carpets of bluebells or other wildflowers that defy imagination.

THIS PAGE: Spring is made for window boxes. Spoilt for
choice, pack your boxes with all the spring colours you can.
These blooms are usually quite low, so make it a cheery carpet
flowing out of your window. Think colour and vibrancy.

hyacinth duvet and pillows

Hyacinths are easy, quick spring blooms. The seemingly
boring little brown bulb can produce a succulent,
powerfully scented, many-petalled bloom in pink, white
or blue. They remind me of feather dusters! Inspired
by the hyacinth's complementing colours of blue/lilac
and pink, I thought how lovely it would be to fall
asleep amid pastel petals. The cover and pillowcases
would be a labour of love, though, as they would be
made up of overstitched linen, with swirling flower
stitches forming a rich and dense hyacinth texture.

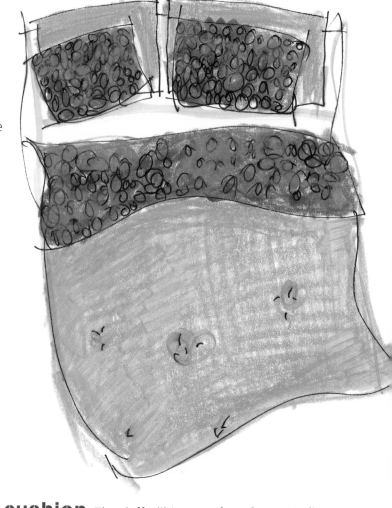

daffodil cushion The daffodil is one of my favourite flowers,
with its simple beauty and a scent that conjures up nostalgic memories of my
childhood in Wales and the winter and spring narcissi of Cornwall. Its bloom
also has a joyous yellow colour that never fails to give a sunny and spring-
like effect anywhere in the house, even on the gloomiest of days. The chair
and cushion reflect the happy, bright feeling of the daffodil by using a
mix of check, gingham and flower fabric, and create a lovely spring corner.

MATERIALS

* A cushion pad in any size –
whatever you prefer, but square
really is the best choice for this
* Fabric, preferably strong, good-
quality cotton (you will need twice as
much of the plain as the floral fabric,
plus extra for the ties and turn-in)
* Pins, thread, needles and so on

HOW-TO

1 Sew together the main front floral
fabric and a strip of the plain yellow
to create a finished square the same
size as your cushion pad, plus a 1.5cm
(⅝in) seam allowance all round.
2 Cut out the back in plain fabric to
the size of the cushion, adding a
1.5cm (⅝in) seam allowance all round.
3 Make up four ties about 25cm
(10in) long.
4 With right sides facing, place the
front and back together. Stitch three
sides of the cushion cover, leaving
one side open. Pin the ties in place

along the edge of the opening.
5 Cut a 10cm (4in) wide band to the
length of the opening's circumference,
plus seam allowance. Stitch together
along the short ends to create a loop.
6 With right sides facing, place the
loop along the opening's edge to
cover the ties, then machine-stitch
around opening to secure in place.
7 Turn the cushion cover through to
the right side, turning the facing
band to the inside of cushion cover
to complete.
NOTE: if possible, overlock all raw
edges before completing the cover.

spring chair cover

Wherever this chair and its cover go, a little corner of spring appears. The covers are made up of a patchwork of gingham and check fabric, stitched together contrasting on the seat, arms, back panel and footstool cushion. Its fresh daffodil-yellow colour is equivalent to the word BOING! In other words, very springy indeed.

a spring table A simple flower arrangement, such as blossom branches or an enormous bucket of daffodils, sets off a spring table setting perfectly. Use complementary fabrics to achieve a fresh, cheerful look and give the table a strong seasonal feature. Candy-striped bunting brings it all together and is really easy to make. Cut paper bags into triangles and staple over a length of string.

fresh spring table linen

Scraps of fabric in zingy colours, fresh florals and cheeky patterns with lots of life and optimism will do nicely for napkins and tablecloths, while pretty ribbons in toning colours and contrasting patterns add a finishing touch tied around napkins and cutlery (flatware).

lettuce cushion Lettuces always make me laugh. They look like little green volcanic eruptions, or green frilly pants. They are a lovely sight and look even more delightful in rows. I saw this crushed-velour bright green cushion in a store and immediately interpreted it as a lettuce or bed of lettuces. Pop a couple of lettuce cushions on your sofa, and you will have a little salad to nod off on.

growing door box

This is really a little window box, but I rather fancied the idea of it being on the front door, always there to greet you and your guests with seasonal cheer. Choose scented plantings if you can. It is much nicer to get a lovely waft of something like lavender or pinks. Whatever is in season, but the headier the better.

spring window-box plants
narcissi * daffodils * tulips * crocus * snowdrops * forget-me-nots * various grasses * bluebells * cowslips * fritillarias

spring indoor cut plants narcissi * daffodils * tulips * catkins from hazel and alder * hyacinths * anemones * lilacs * irises * hellebores * euphorbia * bluebells

blooming eiderdown This lovely, luxurious bed throw has a patchwork effect, but is more eiderdown-like, thick, fresh and cottony – hence the duvet (continental quilt) instead of the more usual wadding found in patchwork quilts. Most important, however, are the flower buds 'growing' out of the quilt, making you feel as if you are enveloped by blooms. On a practical note, once you have inserted the duvet into your finished cover, slip-stitch the opening closed, then stitch every block of four squares, positioning a stay stitch through all the layers to keep the quilt in place and add definition.

MATERIALS

* A feather duvet (continental quilt) – single is a good size for this
* Various fabric scraps in a mixture of checks, gingham, floral prints, big and small scale (you will use overs of this fabric to make your flowers)
* Fabric for the backing in a matching or complementary colour and pattern to the front
* Felt for the leaves, if required
* Pins, thread, needles and so on

HOW-TO

1 To make the flowers, cut out strips of fabric in the colours you fancy, cutting strips of different sizes for various-sized blooms.

2 Fold a strip in half along its length, turn the raw edges in, then lightly gather along the bottom edge and pull up the centre to form a flower. When you are happy with the shape of the bloom, secure it with stitching.

3 Make as many flowers as you like, and stitch their bases on to the quilt where you want. Make little felt cut-out leaves if you get carried away!

the lawn carpet The lawn provides one of the fundamental inspirations of the outside-inside concept. It is one of the most natural, normal and everyday sights; whether it be in your back garden, in a park or in a field, we see it nearly every day in one shape or another. Not only is a 'lawn' carpet hard-wearing and spill-hidingly practical, but it is also beautiful.

the lawn carpet As peculiar as it may seem
to have a lawn-green carpet, it is in reality quite a natural
and obvious floor covering. As the idea developed, it
seemed right for the carpet to 'grow' along the hallway,
up the stairs to the second floor and then fill the
bedrooms with a rich, grassy lusciousness.

Spring is the only season that sounds just like it is … springy! You could also call it 'boing', 'bounce', 'yippee' or 'hurrah'. This season is a joyous time of fresh beginnings, and all that is in your home should reflect this.

floral fairy lights I was thinking about the flowers that twine around a bench and fence at my family home. It made me think about how wonderful it would be to have little spring flowers entwined around my headboard. I liked the idea of falling asleep beneath heady night-scented stock blooms, or any blooms at all really … so I decided to introduce glowing blooms. Delightful.

cloche with snowdrop lighting

Snowdrops are delicate symbols of spring. The way
I thought best to represent these little treasures is by
re-creating them in fairy-light form. This looks good
on an occasional table or even as a centrepiece for a
spring table. It's so simple. Scrunch up white fairy lights
(berry ones are good, with dark green wiring), then
tuck them up in a bundle underneath a glass cloche.
Plug in, turn on and, bingo, luminous snowdrops!

soft terracotta 'pot' cushions

I have lots and lots of terracotta plant pots, stacked outside in the backyard. I like the look of them, especially the old ones. They are all lined up higgledy-piggledy on a rickety wooden shelf. The cushions here are based on these pots. I like the idea of making 'soft' terracotta pots, a bit tidier and newer looking, but you get the gist. I have used as true a terracotta colour as I could get with the fabric. I found that good felt is perfect and very hard-wearing, too.

MATERIALS

* Boxed feather cushion pads – you can either make these yourself (a palaver) or buy them or have them made to suit your needs. Get them made if you can, for a professional finish

* Terracotta-coloured fabric (I used felt for mine, and was delighted with the results – it is thick, not too flimsy or thin, but also not too cardboardy)

* Piping (optional)

* Pins, thread, zippers (optional)

HOW-TO

1 Cut out the top and bottom parts of the cushion fabric to match your pad size, adding a 1.5cm (⅝in) seam allowance on all sides.

2 Cut out the strips that form the sides of the cushion cover, adding a 1.5cm (⅝in) seam allowance on all sides.

3 With right sides facing, stitch the strips together to form continuous bands. Insert piping, if you wish, then machine-stitch the bands to the cover tops. Repeat with the bottom parts, leaving one side open.

4 Turn through and insert the pads into the covers, then slip-stitch to close (alternatively you can insert zippers at the rear of your cushion covers for a zipper opening).

5 If you want to emphasize the pot a little more, top-stitch all the sides using a machine top-stitch.

spring fabrics good-quality crisp cottons ✳ painted organzas and muslins (cheesecloth) ✳ yellow, pink, blue, spring green, violet and brown gingham for spring blooms ✳ fine lime-green velvets and needle corduroys for spring lawns, leaves and shoots ✳ ribbons and felts for catkins and buds

summer

Summer is a fruity and flowery jumbly season of all things wearing their most fancy clothes. Temperatures rise, and the days are lighter, longer. Blossom turns to fruit, and summer's harvest begins … warm, full and hopeful.

Glorious summer is a riot of colour, texture, scent and taste. This is the time of the year when anything goes, really, and you will be faced with endless choice. Flowers, fruits and mature plants are everywhere. In London it can get hot, too hot for my little plot, which needs all the windows open and a bevy of fans. It just is too dirty, dusty and grimy to stay in the city, too busy and full of tourists on the routes to the seaside, and, when you get there, there is no space. It is a funny old time. You need friends or family in high, deserted places or a cottage rental in a remote seaside location. Travelling down to Cornwall is the answer for me, or my family's garden as it is impossible to stay out of, in contrast to my piddly little urban roof terrace and backyard.

summer colours
multicolours * pinks * reds * yellows * oranges * dark, lush greens * blues * purples * orange * every blooming thing

OPPOSITE: This jumble of a window box uses a mix of quite traditional, seasonally identifiable plantings: strawberries, sea thrift, grass, night-scented stock and pinks. A heady mix and rather eclectic, but it looks, smells and tastes lovely.

caterpillar draught dodger Living in an old house means creaks, rattles and lots of draughts. On some windy nights in my particular old house, I could feel (and hear) the wind whipping in through the doors from the back garden, up the stairs, and through my hair ... I find that this chubby caterpillar solves the problem. He slumps himself across my door now, blocking any cheeky draughts, while at the same time looking rather dashing.

MATERIALS

* A feather bolster cushion (as long as you require to block your draught) – these can be found at good haberdashery stores or in the haberdashery section of larger department stores
* Caterpillar-coloured fabric (choose one that is bright and jolly – I used a light green velvet)
* Matching thread

HOW-TO

1 Make a fitted cover to fit your bolster cushion, insert the pad and slip-stitch to close.
2 To make the bolster look like a caterpillar, make lines of running stitch using cotton thread around sections of the bolster at equal intervals. Do not tie off the ends.
3 Ruche up tightly by pulling on both thread ends of the running stitch, securing on the underside of the bolster to make the segments effective.
4 Alternatively, use strips of ribbon for a more glamorous feature, simply tying the ribbon in place.

summer window-box plants

foxgloves (horribly poisonous – wear gloves when handling) * lupins (fabulous fireworks in the window box) * alliums (rather proud pom-poms) * climbing sweet peas (heady summer scent) * sweet williams (traditional and aromatic) * snapdragons (bonbons on sticks) * nasturtiums (luxurious orange rampancy) * shrub and climbing roses, but only if you want them for ever * marigolds (very jolly) * poppies (nice and simple) * hollyhocks (amazing!) * pinks (a bit peaky in colour, but subtle with a wonderful smell) * fruits and vegetables * herbs (perfect for summer salads)

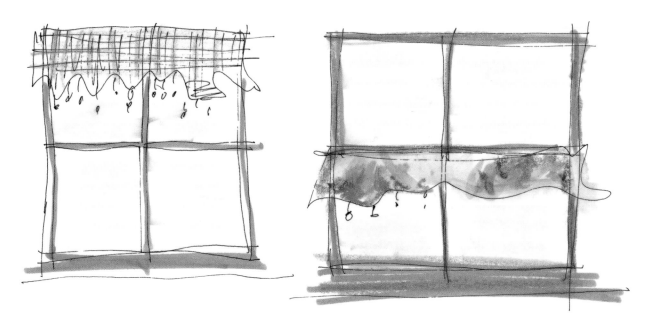

meadow curtains
These curtains (drapes) are of the most wonderful fabric, a scrunchy linen, with a beautiful, almost Enid Blytonesque floral print. They represent the classic bunch of wild garden or meadow flowers I would love to have in my bedroom all year round. The soft, pale, chalky blue melts into the blue colour of the walls. The curtains are extra thick and long to block out city noise and light, with exaggerated large box pelmets to make them larger than life. I lie in bed at night trying to identify the individual blooms.

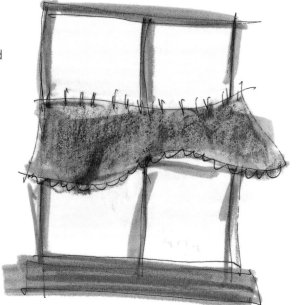

peeking half-panels
These cheeky panels that hang from the halfway mark of the window instantly turn you into a nosy neighbour. They can be made in any fabric – simple gingham in a seasonal colour looks lovely with a pom-pom or gorgeous trim to contrast with its simplicity; a rich floral fabric is always a treat in summer; or be authentic and use a textural, hedge-like fabric.

green-leaf bathroom into purple-flower bedroom

These two rooms are on one floor of a Georgian house. Each floor ran around a huge atrium and flowed with colours suggested by the wonderful garden outside – in particular, a delicate purple flower which bloomed the most fabulous violet-purple in the summer. It inspired the bedroom colour palette. I wanted the en suite to be the green of the foliage. Looking from the bathroom to the bedroom as the picture shows, you can see the whole blooming effect!

THIS PAGE: Reading all about the snapdragon in my vibrant hot-pink chair, propped up by the essential summer deckchair cushion.

Summer fireworks – what a treat! In my house I have plant fireworks – foxgloves, snapdragons, lupins, delphiniums and alliums, all reaching out to the sky with rockets of colour.

summer window

Instead of blocking out the lovely bright light with a blind (shade), this map makes an uninteresting window quirky and looks wonderful in the summer sunshine. The jaunty bunting is made of large triangles of coloured tissue paper. Simply fold the top edge over the string, and glue or staple it in place. The idea came from various road trips to seaside towns, headscarves, garden parties and cream teas ... Pip, pip!

maze rug This textured

rug creates a feature in a rather grand house. It represents all the formality of a near-stately home, but has a witty twist in that the maze is indoors and made of hedge-green wool.

deckchair blind

Deckchair fabric is great – lots of colours and stripes, all very jolly and hard-wearing. I have used an old piece of deckchair fabric to make a simple panel blind which slips on to hooks in the window frame. Excess fabric with some other scraps of stripy fabric make up the cushion, which looks superb on the vibrant pink chair. It follows the same principles as the spring daffodil cushion on page 84, without the ties.

summer fabrics lush lawn-like felts * wools * embroidered panels on muslin (cheesecloth), organza and cotton * nostalgic floral fabrics * scrunchy, thick linens, vintage and crisply new * silks * big-checked ginghams * fine ginghams

wallpaper-rose blind

This floor of the house is blooming. Each room has a garden rose or flower on the wall representing a garden flower outdoors. In this particular room, the red-pink garden rose is a lovely full bunch on the wallpaper. Instead of just matching the curtains to the same print, as is safe and 'normal', experimentation with the print led to a single rose image from the wallpaper being blown up in size using an overhead projector and a pattern being created from it. Appropriate-coloured fabrics were then appliquéd onto a simple Roman blind (shade) to show this same rose, reflecting the wallpaper as a bigger, softer image. This is a very tricky procedure and one best left to a professional. It is a lot of work, but the results make a huge impact in an otherwise seemingly typical flowery bedroom.

summer indoor cut plants foxgloves (but remember these girls are dangerous without care and learning) ✳ lupins in big vases (my favourite!) ✳ sweet peas (you can never have enough of these) ✳ sweet williams (traditional-looking and smelling nice, in an earthenware jug or pitcher) ✳ alliums (grand and simple – put lots in a tall glass vase) ✳ snapdragons (amazing flowers which really do snap) ✳ nasturtiums (prolific creepers with lovely leaves – use little jars) ✳ buddleia (tall and grand and common as muck) ✳ shrub and climbing roses (Barbara Cartland level of use) ✳ jasmine (yummy smell) ✳ honeysuckle (ditto) ✳ wisteria (big blooms on short stems, with a short life) ✳ poppies (plain and simple – tall vase) ✳ gladioli (big, big, big, tall and elegant) ✳ clematis (single bloom – in cup, pot or glass) ✳ marigolds (orange festival – big metal tub) ✳ pinks (in the bathroom and by the bed) ✳ hollyhocks (English country garden bloom) ✳ lavender (a bedside must)

painted organza panels The theory behind these lovely blinds (shades) is that, even if you live opposite a construction site or large block of offices, look out on to a building crane or just on to a typical urban eyesore, with these panels you will be looking at your favourite garden scene instead. I wanted to peer out into a garden of tall lupins, but the options are endless. Hedging, roses, lavender, peonies, delphiniums or snapdragons – you can choose anything you want that represents the nonurban and very garden-like. You could even have prize runner beans if that is what tickles your fancy.

MATERIALS
✳ Sheer fabric – organza, light cotton canvas or muslin (cheesecloth)
✳ Acrylic paint in colours of your choice for your flowers or plants
✳ Wooden dowelling rod
✳ C hooks for attaching to the window frame

HOW-TO
1 Take the window measurement, then cut the sheer fabric to the size of the window, adding 3cm (1¼in) on both sides and the bottom edge, and 5cm (2in) at the top.
2 Turn and stitch a double 1.5cm (⅝in) hem at the sides and bottom of the panel. Now turn the top down 1cm (½in), then turn again another 4cm (1½in) to form a casing at the top.
3 Press all hems.
4 Paint your panel!
5 Insert the dowelling rod through the casing hem.
6 Attach the C hooks to the window frame, then hang the panel on to the hooks using the dowelling.

rose chandelier This lighting feature is an idea based on a climbing rose clambering and entwining round a gazebo, creating an intense floral display. I have used a mixture of fairy lights which wrap around a spiral wire frame. This has to be really packed with lights to produce a dense effect. Plug the lights into the nearest electrical socket, and use green wire or twine to give the chandelier a prickly-stalk-and-thorn detail.

rose-bush sofa The sofa pictured here sits in a garden room looking down a garden path surrounded by rose bushes. A very good rose-print fabric has been used to cover a boxy-shaped sofa. The fabric makes it – gorgeous and chintzy, with the roses looking so effective that they seem the same as the ones outside.

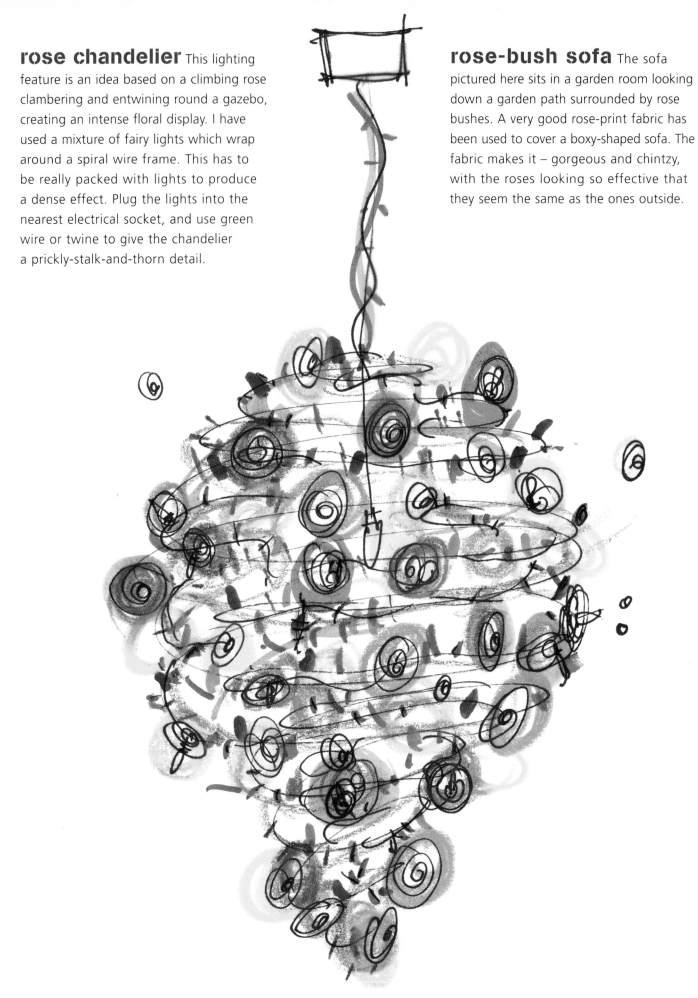

autumn

Autumn (fall) in many ways reminds me very much of spring, in that its arrival hits you with a sudden realization one day. As in spring, it can feel very autumny one day, when only the day before it was quite clearly summer. True autumn cannot be mistaken; it is just what you want after all that blooming frolicking in the sunshine.

autumn window-box plants
fruits ✳ vegetables ✳ herbs and general foliage ✳ branching and twigs ✳ dahlias ✳ autumn crocus

It has a lot to offer, with some splendid celebrations, but I think its essences are smell and colour.

Autumn is damp, musty, smouldering, rotting, warm, fruity, ripe and woody. A particularly nostalgic smell for me is the smell of fires – garden fires and log fires at home. Smells can do wonderful things. And for all the obvious death going on in this season, autumn expresses the most flamboyant exit.

My other autumn influences are many and all rooted in childhood. I have a robust catalogue of memories to build a lifetime of wonderful autumns in my very uncountry-based home in London and be quite content. Conkers, roasting chestnuts, bonfires and fireworks parties, Halloween, apple windfalls and toffee apples … I have a harvest of fruity ideas.

THIS PAGE: This is the turning point of summer to autumn as you can see – the sea thrift is still lingering. The grass is dying out, but I have crammed a selection of pumpkins and gourds in the box to make it look as if they were harvested there from the street outside. It is a very effective autumn display.

autumn fabrics

shiny black satin ✳ thick black felt ✳ black-and-white stripes and checks ✳ seasonal ticking ✳ orange canvas ✳ velvet ✳ mohair ✳ chunky brown woollens ✳ corduroys ✳ tweed

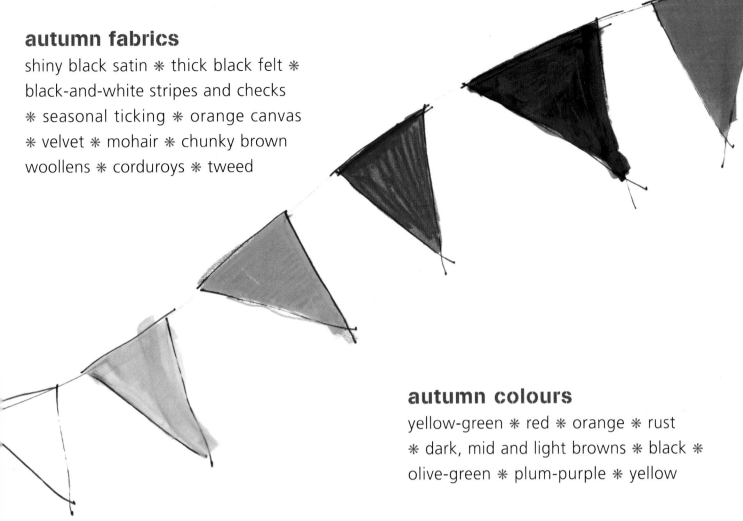

autumn colours

yellow-green ✳ red ✳ orange ✳ rust ✳ dark, mid and light browns ✳ black ✳ olive-green ✳ plum-purple ✳ yellow

2D pumpkin blind

This is basically meant to be a flat or almost 2D pumpkin – what a pumpkin would look like if it were deflated. The blind (shade) is a simple panel construction that rolls up with ribbons. I have used orange velvet with a hessian (burlap) backing to give the effect of the pumpkin nestling in straw.

MATERIALS

✳ Pumpkin-orange fabric (velvet is good for this as it has a slight sheen)
✳ Hessian (burlap)
✳ Wadding – use either folded lengths of interlining or polyester wadding (about 350–400g (12–14oz))
✳ Orange satin ribbon and dark green twine
✳ C hooks for attaching to the window frame

HOW-TO

1 Measure your window, then cut both the pumpkin-orange fabric and hessian to the measurement, adding a seam allowance of 1.5cm (⅝in) on both sides and the bottom edge of both fabrics, and 2.5cm (1in) at the top.
2 With the right sides of the fabrics facing, stitch the sides and bottom, leaving an opening at the top.
3 Turn the panel through so the right sides of the fabrics are now facing out.
4 Stitch down through the panel at various intervals to form channels – these represent sections of the pumpkin.
5 Stuff the channels with wadding to create a 3D ridged effect in your finished blind.
6 To finish the top of the blind, overlock the raw edges.
7 Fold over the 2.5cm (1in) top opening and slip-stitch to the reverse side of the panel to secure.
8 To make up the stalk ties, twist lengths of twine to create loops to hook over the window hooks, then hand-stitch them into position on the reverse side of the blind's top.
9 Hang the blind using the C hooks. To roll it up, slip the orange satin ribbon around the whole panel, and tie it up to the height at which you want your blind to be.

MATERIALS

* A quantity of healthy *Physalis* branches, with lanterns in a strong orange colour and a mixture of sizes; you need as many as you think is right for your wall space
* Wire, thread (coloured or clear), twine or ribbon – thin and flexible but strong (I used gold florist's wire)
* Tacks, fine nails or adhesive tape

chinese lantern wall hanging

I have always loved lanterns, especially paper ones. Their glow and fragility are a delight. The Chinese lantern plant, or *Physalis*, reminds me of a paper lantern. *Physalis* is available for the autumn months and into winter, and can be bought at most good florists. This effective autumn decorative idea is a little fiddly at first, but you will soon get the hang of it. You can be quite flexible with where you want to put it, be it the wall or as a partition. It is a little fragile, though, and will not take being walked into or past a lot. Depending on how you want the hanging to look, you could have an invisible thread, which gives the effect of the lanterns 'floating' in midair, or a feature thread.

HOW-TO

1 Gently remove the lanterns, complete with their stalks, from the branches.

2 Cut as many varying lengths of wire or thread as you will need to cover your chosen area.

3 Wrap the wire or thread around a stalk or, if using wire, make a little stitch in the side of the lantern and twist the wire to lock the lantern in place.

4 Repeat this method as often as you want for your lengths, and for as many lengths as you need to make the hanging look healthy and not sparse.

5 Hang the lengths in position using fine nails, tacks or adhesive tape, spacing them at regular intervals and randomly staggering the long and short lengths.

Autumn smells of comfort and warmth, bonfires and damp leaves; feels like snuggles and cuddles, long wraparound scarves and walks in wellies; and tastes like toffee and nuts, hedgerow fruits and homemade beer. Yum!

blackberry hedge throw

I had the idea for this after seeing the most wonderful crocheted woollen fabric in a shop in Soho, London. It was deep blue-black and looked just like a blanket of blackberries. It got me thinking about this autumn throw, with some felt and satin leaves stitched on and prickly twine threads to complete the scene. No stains, either!

bonfire cushion

This cushion is essentially a felt-panelled cushion cover with lots of appliquéd twigs and different fabrics overstitched with different threads. A lovely idea, but one you would need to start on the year before for the following year, as it is a lot of work.

toffee-apple cushion

A big, cylindrical cushion with half toffee-coloured fabric and half red-apple satin, this is another autumn inspiration. The stretchy big toffee apple on the edge of your sofa will make it deliciously inviting. Make the stick out of curled-up stiff felt.

chinese lantern fairy lights

My friend Tim, the world's greatest florist, came up with this idea with me while we were on a shoot. Inspired by autumn, it needed a lighting feature. We had already made the Chinese lantern wall hanging and had lots of little lanterns left over, so popping the little paper shades over the lights fixed on the ceiling seemed a sweet idea. They glowed all autumn long and it was a wrench to take them down, they were so gorgeous.

autumn indoor cut plants

dahlias (glorious tall explosions in tin tanks or tin vases) * hydrangeas * chrysanthemums * crab apples (hanging, threaded, in glass jugs or pitchers) * Virginia creeper (draped over pictures, hanging on doors with orange gingham tie) * ivy (as above) * horse chestnut (leaves as wreaths or hangings; nuts as hangings) * vegetables, especially pumpkin * herbs (clusters for hanging and ridding of evil) * branches and twigs

nature table I have fond memories of nature tables from my childhood, when I was at primary school in Wales. We would bring in seasonal items – in autumn it would be nuts, leaves, apples and fruits. We would label them and keep adding to the seasonal display. This is a living diary of autumn.

cornish panels My last trip to Cornwall inspired these panels. I was sketching the gorgeous granite paving slabs outside the cottage in which I was staying. There were little weeds and plants growing in between the slabs just like a living jigsaw puzzle. The greys of the granite and greens of the weeds looked so beautiful, I came up with these Cornish panel curtains (drapes), using a patchwork of fabrics – velvets, felts and wools all of the greys and greens. These curtains were exquisitely made by a specialist seamstress. The shapes are odd and random, and have been stitched first with green thread, then in turn stitched on to a thick felted wool.

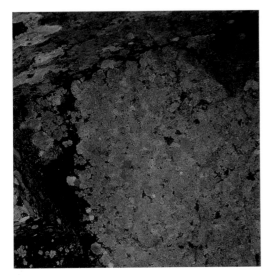

lichen wall treatment I think this wall treatment is a good reflection of the essence of lichen, its vibrancy and fluorescence. It works best in a small room or on a single wall, but try to test your colours and technique on a roll of white lining paper first. This really does help you to get a feel for the way you want it to look.

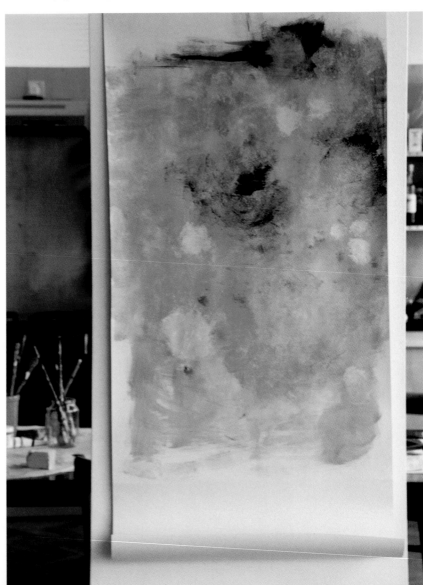

MATERIALS
* An image of some fantastic lichen
* A roll of lining wallpaper
* Different-sized sponges with cut edges and holes cut out
* Acrylic paint in white, black, yellow and green (use fluorescent green and yellow)

HOW-TO
1 Mix your paint to the shades you want on a plate, tray or palette, using your image as a reference and building up the colours slowly. The image will never be as vibrant as the real thing, so up the zing!
2 Dab the sponges very gently in the paint; build up the lichen on the lining paper.
3 If you are happy with your sample, try it out on a wall. But do not rush it.

windy day leaf chandelier

This idea was inspired by autumn leaves and how they frolic ... whether hurling themselves to the ground or are suddenly whipped up by a gust of wind to create a leafy vortex when gathered en masse. I used real leaves for this, simply hooked on to the chandelier framework with florist's wire (see page 118). Use as many or as few as you want, and replace as and when.

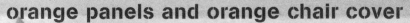

orange panels and orange chair cover

This past year, the entire autumn Halloween season for me was inspired by the humble pumpkin. In fact, you could say it was the 'year of the pumpkin'. In my living room I had a pumpkin chair and stool, an orange mohair throw and these pumpkin panels in a rich orange velvet, simply lined and with stalk ties made of ribbon.

MATERIALS

* Pumpkin-orange fabric (once again I am using velvet for the sheen, but you don't have to …)
* Fabric for lining
* Ribbon for the stalk ties, about 2.5cm (1in) in width, in straw and dark green
* C hooks for attaching to the window frame

HOW-TO

1 Cut your fabric panels to the size of your windows, adding a seam allowance of 1.5cm (¾in) on all sides of both the pumpkin-orange fabric and the lining.
2 Make as many stalk ties as looks good for your window. Gather your ribbon stalk ties and fold them in half. Place them along the top edge of the orange fabric, using a length of each colour per tie and leaving a healthy space between them – it's up to you!
3 Place the lining fabric on top, with the right sides facing.
4 Machine-stitch all sides through all layers, stitching through the ribbons to secure them along the top. Leave an opening of about 5cm (2in).
5 Turn through, and slip-stitch the opening to close.
6 Tie the stalks to the C hooks to hang the blind.

eerie halloween bats in the trees
This project turned out to be one of the easiest, cheapest, most effective and funniest I have ever constructed. I delighted in making the eerie yet cheeky little bats, and I think this makes a very striking seasonal decoration. What's more, these ribbon bats are not too scary. They are really quite cute – far more cool than ghoul.

MATERIALS
* Black, thick-width wired ribbon with a semi-sheen
* Twigs and branches
* A large pot or container (such as a galvanized-iron bucket) for twigs

HOW-TO
1 Cut your ribbon into shortish lengths, experimenting to get the correct bat wingspan (it is better to be generous at this stage to ensure that you do not end up with stubby-winged nocturnal creatures).
2 Arrange the twigs and branches in your container to achieve the look of a leafless tree.
3 Tie a length of ribbon on to a twig or branch wherever you choose. Knot the ribbon twice, then flex the ribbon ends (you may need to trim them to a realistic size), and bend them into a shape resembling bat wings in flight.
4 Repeat to rustle up a gang of bats!

winter

I am always exclaiming that one season or another is my favourite season. Now I think that I am in fact a fraud and actually delight in them all with equal passion – apart from winter, which really, really is my favourite. After all, it has a great big celebration slap bang in the middle of it to distract you from the length and tedium of relentless bleakness – Christmas. Winter is the big brother of seasons, a time for luxury. It gives you space to sit down, snuggle up and think about the next season.

winter window-box plants

Christmas trees (small and well proportioned; one per window, with or without lights) ✳ heather (thick crop of white or red, or green) ✳ snowdrops (dense and snow-like – great with berried shrubs) ✳ aconites ✳ hellebores ✳ white crocus ✳ early iris ✳ cyclamen ✳ various ivies (thick, twisting and intense)

I have never taken to unnatural colours for winter. I cannot bear the thought of modernizing winter, cheering it up with pastels. Nor do I understand why silver and gold have such a grip on the season. For me it is dark and lush, the lighting is very low and the whole season smells fruity and spicy, as if the months themselves were being preserved. You cannot minimize winter – it is simply too big and too hefty.

OPPOSITE: This window box is filled to overflowing with white heather. It grows rampantly and, when in full bloom, it can produce a blanket of white flowers. I wanted to create a snow effect outside my windows, one that I could rely on.

evergreen stamping This hand-printed winter forest for your wall works well on pillars and doors, too. Either buy a rubber stamp or get one made up to the size and shape you desire. Practise on lining paper, and dip into dark green and light green ink to give depth. Make your forest as thick or as sparse as you wish.

evergreen window box I have always put Christmas trees in my window boxes at Christmas. This year I left them quite natural. I wanted the effect to be that of a tree growing out of the window box. I chose good-shaped trees of similar sizes and widths, and made sure that they were well set into the soil. A root helps with this.

Prickly holly, crackling fires, crunchy snow underfoot, satsuma peel everywhere, pine needles in your socks, frosty breath and pink cheeks – wintertime's short, dark, chilly days need to be cheered up with things that twinkle, sparkle and glow.

THIS PAGE: A simple shade, this is in fact a mohair-panel Roman blind that represents a scarf. What I really wanted was to knit a scarf especially for this window, with fringing, too. The knitted wool might stretch, though, so a lining of some sort would be necessary. It would be such a lovely thing – gorgeous stripes of cheery winter shades.

winter wool chair cover

I wanted this chair to have the feeling of thick foliage. Think of fir, ivy and eucalyptus shades. I found a thick upholstery wool that had many different tones within it, giving a dense forest-like appearance. It is a warm and comforting chair, and sits very well in a winter and Christmas setting. Experiment with different evergreen fabrics, velvets and felts with different textures – even a patchwork if you fancy.

log cushion The typical Yuletide log, but this time in cushion form. This is a lovely regular at Christmas, and lies proudly on the evergreen chair. It is a beautiful felt creation. I have used a different-coloured felt for the log ends and pleated the log fabric to create a bark effect. A detachable snow cover is a possible idea, with a robin on for special occasions.

MATERIALS
* Felt for the cushion slip cover, in green for the holly leaf, red for the berry, and browns for the log itself (a dark and a light brown)
* A log-shaped or cylindrical cushion bolster

HOW-TO
1 Calculate the size of the main area of the cushion bolster, as well as the circular ends.
2 Cut out the piece for the main log shape in dark brown felt, and the circular log ends in the lighter brown felt, adding a 1.5cm (⅝in) seam allowance around all of the edges.
3 To create the bark effect on the body of the log, use a machine-stitch pinch pleating of random lengths.
4 Create a cylinder of the dark brown felt, machine-stitching with right sides facing. Next stitch the lighter brown log ends to the ends of the cylinder, leaving an opening to insert the bolster.
5 Turn through, insert the bolster and slip-stitch the opening closed.
6 Make up your holly leaves and berries out of the green and red felt, and attach them to the cushion with a stitch or two.

tweed and berry-red blanket

Influenced by a pair of my dad's old tweed trousers, I wondered about making a tweedy winter blanket, but wanted it to be a bit more jolly and a lot softer. So the contrasting fabric I chose for this project is a soft red fake fur – wintry and cosy, but jolly and luxuriously smooth. It has been well used! This blanket is more complicated than it looks, unfortunately, as it involves making a template because the fur border surrounding the tweed centre panel is mitred. This means the corners are cut on the diagonal so that the finished edging is flat and neat, as in the picture below and just like a store-bought satin-edged woollen blanket.

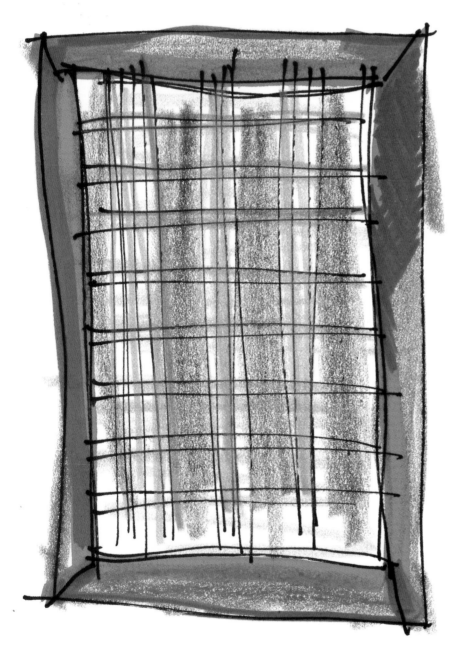

MATERIALS
* Tweed wool, in a good suit-weight fabric – go for browns, greens and reds
* Red fake-fur fabric
* Matching thread

HOW-TO

1 First you must make up a pattern for your blanket. Draw your template out on paper, to scale – basically a large rectangle about 1.2m by 1.5m (48in by 60in). Draw in the mitred borders of 15cm (6in) width. The area in the middle of the blanket is in the tweed, while the back and borders are in the fur fabric.

2 Cut out the pieces of the template (the border pattern will be four pieces, with short edges cut on the diagonal to form the mitred corners). Place each template piece on the relevant fabric, then cut out the fabric to match, remembering to add a 1.5cm (⅝in) seam allowance on all sides.

3 With right sides together, stitch the fur border pieces around the tweed centre to create the blanket front, joining the border pieces together at the corners.

4 With right sides facing, place the finished front panel and the fur back panel together. Stitch around all the sides, leaving an opening of 50cm (20in) along the bottom edge, then turn through and slip-stitch to close.

winter fabrics rich dark brown and green ginghams * velvets * shiny silks in brown, green and olive * linen * felt * wool * mohair * tweed * fake furs * chunky corduroys * stretchy stripy fabric * textured whites

holly-green chair cover

This chair cover using very cheap cotton gingham makes a lovely background for jolly seasonal cushions. Choose a dark, evergreen green for the best effect.

snowfall panels

These panels rely on fabric factor alone. No stitching at all is required – just cutting to size and pinning to the frame of your window or door. The fabric is the inspiration. It is a sheer wool strewn with clusters or balls to create the snowfall effect. It looks as if snow is falling just outside the window.

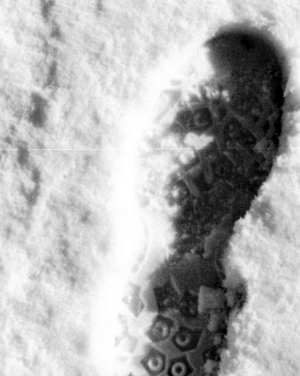

winter indoor cut plants

cyclamen (in pots) ✳ holly (sprigs behind pictures; big, brave jugs (pitchers) and vases) ✳ ivy (clusters for door hangings, tied with ribbon or gingham, over pictures or mantelpieces or climbing up the staircase) ✳ mistletoe (hanging in doorways, or wherever kisses are wanted) ✳ fir (intense vases at bedsides, lit with berry lights in red or green) ✳ heather (lucky gypsy clusters, with green heather for a winter moor effect; small jars) ✳ snowdrops (jam jars, mustard pots or sherry glasses) ✳ aconites (small vases) ✳ hellebores (medium vases, tasteful, refined position) ✳ hawthorn ✳ yew ✳ coloured barks and stems ✳ brambles and thistles ✳ old dried ferns ✳ anemones ✳ Christmas-light flowers (anywhere, any time) ✳ Christmas trees (big in the living room, small in bedrooms, and in the greenhouse/studio, lit as required)

shiny red bauble cushion

This project has nothing whatsoever to do with the outdoors; it is just a cheeky Christmas cushion. I have three of these now, all ready for a giant Christmas tree cushion one day. It is made of a stretchy, shiny satin-like fabric.

MATERIALS

✳ Shiny, stretchy, bauble-type fabric in a bauble colour
✳ Shiny metallic-type fabric for the silver hook top
(you could also choose gold or grey fabric, if you prefer)
✳ An inflatable beach ball
✳ Lining fabric for cushion pad, plus materials for stuffing
✳ Matching thread

HOW-TO

1 Get yourself a normal cheap everyday beach ball – this will be the template for your bauble. Cut the beach ball into eight segments, and make a pattern from the segments.

2 Cut out your fabric using the pattern pieces, adding a 1.5cm (⅝in) seam allowance all round. Machine-stitch the segments together, leaving an opening to enable you to insert the cushion pad.

4 The cushion pad is made in the same way as the cover – beach ball, segments – but the lining fabric is stuffed with feathers, beans, foam or whatever, and sealed tight.

5 Insert the cushion pad into the slip cover.

6 To make the silver top, use the contrasting fabric to represent the bauble top. Make a ribbed and padded 'cuff' strip formed into a band, and secure it to the top of the bauble. Attach a circle of the contrasting fabric to the top to cover the hole.

a winter table Here I have made quite a dark tablecloth in wood-brown linen with pom-pom berries stitched to the corners for holly. The atmosphere is festive but quiet, no glitter or unreal seasonal shades. Rather, the colours used are simple, natural shades – reds, browns, greens and white. I have made holly and ivy napkin wraps with ribbon – no pretence. This makes for an everyday, 'practicalish' table setting.

snowman fridgy cosy

I thought the refrigerator could do with a warm-up … in a cold way. I feel very affectionate towards my fridge now! The face rolls up for access to the fridge, but roll it down and you have your own snowy fella, all in thick, soft, touchable felt, right there in your home, fresh from the garden.

holly bush blind

This shade is a simple representation of a holly bush. Put as many leaves on to the panel as you want your bush to have. Use a lovely soft felt in any green that you fancy.

MATERIALS
* Holly-berry green light felt
* Red pom-poms for the berries
* Light green ribbons for the leaves
* Cord, dowelling, rings and hooks

HOW-TO

1 Cut the green felt to the size of the window, adding a 1.5cm (⅝in) seam allowance to both sides and bottom, with a top heading of about 4cm (1¾in).

2 Make a casing at the top of the blind for the dowelling rod.

3 Stitch pom-pom berries on to the blind, and add ribbon bows in various sizes to the berries.

4 On the reverse side of the blind, sew two sets of plastic rings, placed at equal spaces vertically up the blind. Tie a length of cord to each of the bottom plastic rings.

5 Hang the blind on two C hooks screwed into the window frame.

6 Secure two screw eyes into the window frame in line with the rings. Thread the cords up through the rings on the back of the blind and through the corresponding screw at the top (under the blind).

7 Thread the left-hand cord through the right-hand screw eye and pull the cords together to ruche up the blind.

winter colours

dark green ✳ emerald green ✳
olive ✳ red ✳ white ✳ brown
✳ fairy light neon's ✳ electric
colours ✳ bauble colours ✳
dull battered metals

ribbon holly Ribbon holly is just that:
simple ribbon ties that can wrap around anything
that you want. I have used lots of different types
of ribbon – satin, organza, wide, thin and of
various holly shades. As a feature of the holly,
place a red ribbon and knot it a few times at the
ends. This will give you lovely red berries – use
satin red ribbon for this. I attach the ribbons to
lights to give an extra twinkle.

robin in holly Robin has been about for a few years. He comes out as regular as winter to rest his weary, wiry legs on a branch of holly. He causes no bother, really. Just sits nicely looking cute and evoking the spirit of the season.

snowy lights It never snows when you want it to, so I came up with an indoor snowfall solution, Its delicate flakes are pom-poms hanging tentatively among white fairy lights. At night-time it is quite magical.

MATERIALS
* A selection of fairy lights with black wiring, and good strong, white bulbs
* Pom-pom fringing, in different sizes (available from ribbon stores or haberdashery departments of department stores)

HOW-TO
1 Cluster your fairy lights into whatever snowy fall shape you like and hook onto a window catch or lock. Connect the plug socket to the power.
2 Wrap and entwine the pom-poms around your light, cutting the strips to various lengths to create an effect of different stages of snowfall.
3 Wait until night time and switch on.

index

Figures in *italics* refer to captions.

resources

influences This book is all about things that are all around you, how they make you feel and think. They can be odd and quite ordinary everyday things as well as the extraordinary and downright invigorating. Having original and creative thought is very personal and all about you and the way that you see things. Look up, look down and look all around you, as there is always an inspiration on even the greyest of days, and in the most unexpected places. The things, places and people that have made me think and have funny ideas are weird and wonderful, but important and very precious. These things inspire me to think, and everyone should have a list like this. Make your own – it is great fun and very revealing.

My favourite jumper, cookbooks and people that cook, New York, cheese, eating outside, watching my dogs playing, beautiful skateboards and surfboards, motorbikes, shoes … all of them, gardening at any time, anywhere, Ozzy Osbourne, quiffs and rock and roll dancing, the smell of home, the art of Robert Clarke, satsumas, tinsel, children's books, garden roses, hedgerows, seasonal blooms, Volvos, black-and-white flooring, Tommy Cooper, Cornish cliffs, Devon landscapes, Welsh rain, The Mercer Hotel New York, martinis and margaritas, conkers, seaside, St John Restaurant London, a good frying pan and a sharp knife, my grandma, fish and chips, big, fat art books, Welsh rugby, exhausting walks, birdsong and all my chums.

bathrooms
Aston Matthews
141–147a Essex Road,
London N1 2SN, UK
+44 (0)20 7226 3657
www.astonmatthews.co.uk
Good range of quality fittings.

C P Hart & Sons
Newnham Terrace, Hercules Road,
London SE1 7DR, UK
+44 (0)20 7902 1000
www.cphart.co.uk
Good range of expensive fittings.

Kohler Co.
+1 800 456 4537
www.kohler.com
Leading American manufacturers
of sanitaryware.

The Water Monopoly
16–18 Lonsdale Road,
London NW6 6RD, UK
+44 (0)20 7624 2636
www.watermonopoly.com
Beautiful reclaimed antique
bathroom furniture and fixtures.
Exceptional service.

blooms and plants
Clifton Nurseries
5a Clifton Villas, London W9 2PH, UK
+44 (0)20 7289 7894
www.clifton.co.uk
A good nursery for all your plants
and plantings within London.

Columbia Road Flower Market
Columbia Road, London E2, UK
www.eastlondomarkets.com
Every Sunday morning, 8 am–2 pm.
Over 50 plant and flower stalls.

McQueens
126 St John Street,
London EC1V 4JS, UK
+44 (0)20 7251 5505
www.mcqueens.co.uk
Wow flowers.

**New Covent Garden
Flower Market**
London SW8 5NB, UK
+44 (0)20 7720 2211
www.cgma.gov.uk
Everything that sprouts and
blooms under one huge roof.

drawing and colouring in
The British Rubber Stamp Co. Ltd
3rd Floor Scrutton Street,
London EC2A 4RU, UK
+44 (0)20 7247 1811
Stamps for all.

Stuart R Stevenson
68 Clerkenwell Road,
London EC1M 5QA, UK
+44 (0)20 7253 1693
www.stuartstevenson.co.uk
A lovely art shop.

fabric
British Felt Co.
14 Drakes Mews,
Crownhill, Milton Keynes,
Bucks, MK8 OER, UK
+44 (0)1908 263304
www.britishfelt.co.uk
Huge range of felts.

The Cloth House
98 Berwick Street,
London W1F 0QJ, UK
+44 (0)20 7287 1555
www.clothhouse.com
Magical fabrics.

The Cloth Shop
14 Berwick Street,
London W1F 0PP, UK
+44 (0)20 7287 2881
All cloths.

Colefax and Fowler
39 Brook Street,
London W1Y 2JE, UK
+44 (0)20 7244 7427
Luxury furnishing fabrics.

Donghia Furniture/Textiles Ltd
485 Broadway,
New York, NY 10013, USA
+1 1212 486 1252
www.donghia.com
Wonderful range of textiles, as
well as furniture and accessories.

Fabric Mart
511 Penn Avenue,
Sinking Spring, PA 19608, USA
1 800 242 3695
www.fabricmartfabrics.com
Designer fabrics at great prices.

Ian Mankin
109 Regent's Park Road,
London NW1 8UR, UK
+44 (0)20 7722 0997
All ticking.

Lee Jofa Inc. (USA)
201 Central Avenue South,
Bethpage, NY 11714, USA
+1 516 752 7600
www.leejofa.com
Traditional and innovative fabrics
for interiors.

Lee Jofa/Mulberry (UK)
G18–19, Chelsea Harbour Design
Centre, London SW10 0XE, UK
+44 (0)20 7251 5505
Everything fabric under two roofs.

Ralph Lauren
At selected stores.
+44 (0)20 7235 5010 for outlets
and trade enquiries.
www.polo.com
Exciting American fabrics.

Russell and Chapple
23 Monmouth Street,
London WC2H 9DE, UK
+44 (0)207 836 7521
www.russellandchapple.co.uk
Fantastic canvas.

VV Rouleaux
6 Marylebone High Street,
London W1U 4NJ, UK
+44 (0)20 7224 5179
www.vvrouleaux.com
Incredible ribbons and bows.

flooring
Amazed
Tanfield House, Wighill,
Nr York LS24 8BQ, UK
+44 (0)1937 832813
Rugs beyond your wildest dreams.

Appalachian Woods
1240 Cold Springs Road,
Stuarts Draft, VA 24477, USA
+1 800 333 7610
www.appalachianwoods.com
Antique wood flooring.

The Carpet Library
148 Wandsworth Bridge Road,
London SW6 2UH, UK
+44 (0)20 7736 3664
Carpet in any colour, shape or
form and wonderful service.

Dalsouple
PO Box 140, Bridgewater,
Somerset TA5 1HT, UK
+44 (0)1984 667551
www.dalsouple.com
Rubber flooring.

First Floor
174 Wandsworth Bridge Road,
London SW6 2UQ, UK
+44 (0)20 7736 1123
Lots of floors.

Paris Ceramics
150 East 58th Street, 7th Floor,
New York, NY 10155, USA
+1 1212 644 2785
www.parisceramics.com
Limestone flags, ceramic and
terracotta tiles, and antique flooring.

Tiles and Stones
+1 888 883 3690
www.tilesandstones.com
Ceramic, terracotta and porcelain
tiles, as well as marble, limestone
and granite.

Tower Ceramics
91 Parkway, London NW1 7PP, UK
+44 (0)20 7485 7192
All things tiled and good value.

furniture
And So To Bed
638–640 King's Road,
London SW6 2DU, UK
+44 (0)20 7731 3593
www.andsotobed.co.uk
Beds and mattresses made
to your requirements.

Recline
604 Kings Road,
London SW6 2DX, UK
+44 (0)20 7371 8982
www.recline.uk.com
Sofas and chairs I like.

kitchens
Buyers and Sellers
120–122 Ladbroke Grove,
London W10 5NE, UK
+44 (0)20 7229 8468
White goods, bargain and service.

David L J Babey & Son
www.dbabeyandson.co.uk
+44 (0)1722 711777
www.dbabeyandson.co.uk
Bespoke kitchens – family business.

**National Kitchen & Bath
Association**
687 Willow Grove Street,
Hackettstown, NJ 07840, USA
+1 877 NKBA PRO
www.nkba.org
Directory of certified kitchen
and bathroom designers.

Plain English
Stowupland Hall, Stowupland,
Stowmarket, Suffolk IP14 4BE, UK
+44 (0)1449 774028
www.plainenglishdesign.co.uk
Bespoke kitchens.

Smeg (UK)
Corinthian Court, 80 Milton Park,
Abingdon, Oxon OX14 4RY, UK
+44 (0)1235 861090
www.smeg.com
Sexy refrigerators and ovens.

lighting
Artemide GB
106 Great Russell Street,
London WC1B 3LJ, UK
+44 (0)20 7631 5200
www.artemide.com
Contemporary lighting.

Charles Edwards
582 Kings Road,
London SW6 2DY, UK
+44 (0)20 7736 8490
www.charlesedwards.com
Exquisite antique lighting.

Embassy Electrical
76 Compton Street,
London EC1V 0BN, UK
+44 (0)20 7251 4721
Wonderful, fully stocked
electrical shop.

Flos (UK)
31 Lisson Grove,
London NW1 6UV, UK
+44 (0)20 7258 0600
www.flos.net
Very contemporary lighting.

Flos (USA)
200 McKay Road,
Huntingdon Station, NY 11740, USA
+1 516 549 2745

McCloud Lighting
Showroom 19/20, 3rd Floor,
Chelsea Harbour Design Centre,
London SW10 0XE, UK
+44 (0)20 7352 1533
Quality lighting.

Mr Resistor
82 New Kings Road,
London SW6 4LU, UK
+44 (0)20 7736 7521
www.mr-resistor.co.uk
Electric world.

people who make lovely things
Robert Clarke
+44 (0)7703 466697
Beautiful art commissions.

Julie Cockburn
+44 (0)7775 947489
Artist of wonderful things.

Ben Crook
+44 (0)7903 387464
Graphic designer.

Simon Lock
Favonius & Co., 31 Castle Street,
Salisbury, Wiltshire SP1 1TT, UK
+44 (0)1722 412391
www.flavonius.co.uk
Lovely architects.

Alex Panter
+44 (0)7957 435738
Master craftsman furniture maker.

Melanie Sauzé
+44 (0)7958 475170
Greatest hands that sew and
make soft things.

Brad Yendle
Design Typography, Studio 8,
1st Floor, 2–4 Southgate Road,
London N1 3JJ, UK
+44 (0)20 7812 9609 or
+44 (0)7944 519 784
studio@designtypography.com
www.designtypography.com
Graphic designer.

salvage
Architectural Salvage Inc.
3 Mill Street, Exeter, NH 03833, USA
+1 603 773 5635
www.oldhousesalvage.com
Everything from furniture to
doors and hardware.

Lassco
St Michael's Church,
Mark Street (off Paul Street),
London EC2R 4ER, UK
+44 (0)20 7739 0448
www.lassco.co.uk
Reclamation furniture supermarket.

Salvage Web
www.salvageweb.com
An online service for searching
the worldwide architectural
salvage market.

special things
Bisque
244 Belsize Park,
London NW6 4BT, UK
+44 (0)20 7328 2225
www.bisque.co.uk
Radiators that look really good.

Celestial Buttons
54 Cross Street, London N1 2BA, UK
+44 (0)20 7226 4766
Buttons in all shapes and sizes.

Converse trainers
www.converse.com
Best trainers (sneakers) in the world.

Gardener's
149 Commercial Street,
London E1 6BJ, UK
+44 (0)20 7247 5119
All kinds of bags, fantastic
selection.

Home to be
70 Amwell Street,
London EC1R 1UU, UK
+44 (0)20 7833 3611
Stylish home goods from Italy;
lovely owners!

The National Trust
Holiday Booking Office,
PO Box 356, Melksham,
Wiltshire SP12 8SX, UK
+44 (0)8704 5844221
www.nationaltrust.org.uk
Fantastic places to stay and
be inspired.

walls
Akzo-Nobel
Hollins Road, Darwin,
Lancs BB3 0BG, UK
+44 (0)1254 704951
Wallpaper and Anaglypta.

Bradbury & Bradbury Art
Wallpaper
PO Box 155, Benicia, CA 94510, USA
+1 707 746 1900
www.bradbury.com
More than 140 historic
wallpaper patterns.

Cabot Stains
33360 Central Avenue,
Union City, CA 94587, USA
+1 800 877 8246
www.cabotstain.com
Wood paints, stains and finishes.

Colefax and Fowler
39 Brook Street,
London W1Y 2JE, UK
+44 (0)20 7244 7427
Traditional quality printed wallpaper.

The Old-Fashioned Milk
Paint Company
436 Main Street, Groton,
MA 01450, USA
+1 978 448 6336
www.milkpaint.com
Paints for interiors and furniture
with a timeworn feel.

Old Village Paints
PO Box 1030,
Fort Washington, PA 19034, USA
+1 610 238 9001
www.old-village.com
Authentic eighteenth- and
nineteenth-century paint colours.

Papers and Paints
4 Park Walk, London SW10 0AD, UK
+44 (0)20 7352 8626
www.papers-paints.co.uk
Any colour paints

windows and doors
Original Door Specialists
93 Endwell, Brockley Cross,
London SE4 2NS, UK
+44 (0)20 7252 8109
Lots of doors.

Velux Windows
Woodside Way, Glenrothes East,
Fife, Scotland KY7 4ND, UK
+44 (0)1592 772211
www.velux.co.uk
Windows in the sky.

wonderful stores
After Noah
121 Upper Street,
London N1 1QP, UK
+44 (0)20 7359 4281
www.afternoah.com
Retro old-school furniture.

Castle Gibson
106a Upper Street,
London N1 1QN, UK
+44 (0)20 7704 0927
www.castlegibson.co.uk
Full of original restored furniture.
Wonderful service.

The Conran Shop
Michelin House, 81 Fulham Road,
London SW3 6RD, UK
www.conran.com/shop
+44 (0)20 7589 7401
Conran quality control.

IKEA
www.ikea.co.uk
www.ikea-usa.com
Visit the website to locate a
store near you.

John Lewis
Oxford Street, London W1A 1EX, UK
+44 (0)20 7629 7711
www.johnlewis.com
The best store in the world
for everything.

Liberty
214–220 Regent Street,
London W1R 6AH, UK
+44 (0)20 7734 1234
www.liberty.co.uk
Ye olde England and beyond.

Target
+1 612 304 6073
www.target.com
A national retail chain with
affordable furniture and furnishings.

The Terence Conran Shop
407, East 59th Street,
New York, NY 10022, USA
+1 866 755 9079
www.conran.com
Extensive selection of upholstery,
furniture, lighting, textiles and
home accessories.

Workbench
1 800 736 0030
www.workbenchfurniture.com
Modern furniture and storage.

acknowledgments

There is no doubt that this book has come about purely because of the wonderful people and goings-on around me. It is a book all about inspiration. The following are all-inspiring to me, have enabled me to write, draw and have ideas about things. It has been an adventure, and without these special people it would never have made it out of the seed packet!

Tim at McQueen's for knowing just what I needed, and being so kind and generous; Melanie Sauzé for knowing what I mean with very little explanation and never letting me down (such immaculate work!); Justin at The Water Monopoly, for being a gentleman; Simon at Favonius for helping me understand the hard stuff; Mum and Dad for home and gardens; everyone at Origin Communications; Amanda Culpin; Brad Yendle for wonderful typography and grim single-mindedness; Ben Crook for enthusiasm for rock; Jonathan Ellery for Cornwall; Auntie Pattie for being naturally stylish; Vince Frost for being Vince Frost; Geoff Fowl at St Martins for teaching me to look more; Jeff Palmer for encouraging me to learn; Bert and Mabel for making things hairy but happy; Chi, Zia, Valerie, Siobhán and Lorraine at Conran Octopus for being brave; Jonathan Rose for good eyes; KT for good ears; everyone at Moving Brands for most things; Big Girl for always making me laugh; and Robert Clarke and his wonderful parents Joan and Jim for always caring. Thank you.

Remembering Peter Stobbs for his love of life and books, and my little Bill, who, had he still been here, would have stayed by my side while I wrote and sketched, until I had finished x